# STRENGTH FROM WITHIN

## Vol. I

### O.E. Simon

CANADA ♦ GOLDEN BELL ♦ MCMXCVIII

Copyright 1998
ISBN 0-9683504-1-0

Drawing by Mrs. C. Gleed
Jacket design by K. Laninga


Published by:

*In Canada*:    Golden Bell Publishing House Inc.
P.O. Box 2680
Grand Forks, B.C.  VOH IHO

*In U.S.*:    Golden Bell Publishing House Inc.
P.O. Box 181
Danville, Wash. 99121-0181


PRINTED IN CANADA

# CONTENTS

To
Kirsten

Paula
Apr 12
2007

# About the author

Born in Europe, the author lived through the intense drama of the pre World War II years only to become a young adult faced with the ravages of that war. Seeing man at his worst, immense destruction, human suffering to an unbelievable degree, human cruelty beyond imagination, he too became a victim both mentally and physically. After the war, he proceeded to educate himself and to begin to do what he most loved and that was to write. Receiving the national literary prize in his country for his Durnberger hexameter, his idealism remained yet unfulfilled and he decided to seek out a new land in order to renew his spirits and throw off the shackles of the past.

In North America his dream began to be fulfilled in a most intriguing and unexpected way. Becoming the spiritual leader of the Neo Ch'an Buddhist Temple, he founded a totally new concept of thought and continued to teach over a hundred thousand students. This revolutionary concept was one whose purpose was to unite man through teaching them to "succeed with people and not over them" by creating a special bond which surpassed all religious, racial and national boundaries. He has been described as an individual with an amazing "inner strength", with a unique compassion and idealism - the parents of which were, oddly enough, hardship and struggle. Though fraught with tremendous obstacles over the years, he has continued to prevail, for his idealism and belief in his work propels him forward and each success no matter how small, for each life he might change for the better, is sufficient inspiration for him to continue.

It is this special "inner strength" that in fact gave birth to this book, "Strength from Within" for it was written while his wife was terribly ill and found ten years later on his computer by accident. When asked about the manuscript, he simply said, "Oh, it's just some notes I wrote down. Actually, I had forgotten about them." Well, we hardly know how to express how happy we are that these "notes" were found and we are proud to present them to you in this truly unique and inspiring book.

# STRENGTH FROM WITHIN

# Foreword

♦

# The Struggle

"We are born into that which is and not
that which was or might as yet arrive."

The struggle of man to achieve a superior position before the
ever present forces of nature has taken him all the time he was given
on earth and, in all likelihood, all the time he has been promised in
heaven. Thus learning to adapt, he has become a uniquely equipped
being, so much so as to hold a central position amongst all the
living creatures on this globe.

Man has learned to pass on his experiences in many ways,
communicating over vast periods of time much of that experience to
his followers, his coming generations. His methods of
communication evolved from the most basic to the most fascinating
levels of information exchange: a world wherein the art of
communicating is expanded by means of travel, quick, safe and
efficient, condensing time and distance.

Modern man, as an individual, has also adapted his needs to
some of these mentioned phenomena. He is fairly capable of coping
with his immediate, direct needs (family and friends) and relates to
the expectations which arrive from these needs; at least, he hopes
to know that some reward, some benefit, should be there waiting to

provide for not only his needs but much more his wants.

He is being informed of the latest occurrences close to his abode as well as in the most distant locations on this globe. Instant information offers sound and pictorial reality arriving in his living room with undiminished impact. Modern day man shoulders a gigantic amount of responsibility: one which is closest to him by location and feeling and another one which is remote, far removed from his capability to assist, removed from his direct influence. Yet, both spheres will strike his emotions with an equally realistic fervor.

A remarkable struggle thus evolves inside of each and every human being, varying only in intensity from one person to the next. Different regions involve the human being with different problems, establishing pronounced and specific interests for the citizens.

Cultural barriers find their origin somewhere in time and space and in the fact that man was not always as well acquainted with his counterpart as he seems to be today. Differences in looks and appearance, colour and outlook are much more readily understood as the universities of the world bring their young followers together, equipping them with information pertaining to each other's origin, culture and aim, with the intent of sharing the globe rather than dividing it: the latter being an unwelcome pastime of bygone generations during which the maps of this world were being drawn with little concern for the common future of mankind.

Man's interactions are directed by his interests, benefit and threats toward his benefit which spur these concerns. The severity of such interaction or lack of it will stimulate, either negatively or positively, the relationships amongst his kind. Family disorder, national or international disorder, therefore, have a common denominator anchored deeply within the emotional nature of man.

Neo Ch'an thought is based upon Buddhist tradition whenever physical as well as mind training is taught. The mind training must remain free of mind domination and allow the student to find the way on his own. This involves struggle and at times disappointment, while at the very same time it offers the glory of victory by understanding that one can overcome the worst type of human error, an ingredient of which experience is made for a better understanding of our very own faults. The Temple is identified standing against the rising sun over which the silhouettes of three birds are passing: one bird being of the past, the centre one representing the present and the third one, the highest flying of them all, the future, reminding man that he must have enough courage and wisdom to secure this future for his kind as yet to come.

**We are born into that which is and not that which was or might as yet arrive**. From this observation alone may we trace our errors and misfortunes or, moreover, the greatness of our leaders or lack within them, for they should understand the implication which rests within this simple observation, one which appears to even have succeeded in evading the searching minds of modern scientists, the ones who are concerned with the emotional well-being of their entrusted peoples. History, therefore, must be relearned. If it can be achieved that history can be presented in all its splendour and horror and if it can also be accomplished by our educators and scientists, political as well as religious leaders, that the errors of history, that segment of time in which we did not live, can be brought back to life for the students to see in theory alone, the real experience of war might finally vanish from the earth.

O.E. Simon
July 23, 1998

*iii*

# Chapter I

♦

# Lasting Success

"...the structural, emotional make-up to succeed does not lie in the finding of wealth but in the happiness which comes from the realization to act...."

The shrinking of the globe, boosted by modern techniques and inventions both in travel and communication, has brought about a new era for mankind. China remains just hours away from any continent as well as India or Iran (Persia) can reach each other's shore in only but a few hours. Though man has overcome the severing distance of space, he has not as yet learned to cope with such new situations where, in fact, opposing philosophies, cultures and religions find themselves confronted by a very different challenge. In the face of this sudden modernization, nations have tried to defend themselves from the "culture shock" caused by such encounters in various ways, some trying to adapt to the new times while others, instead of simply dwarfing such attempts, rather elect to condemn them outright; thus plunging their civilizations back in time into the Middle Ages, preferring to contain free thought by controlling the minds of their entrusted peoples. The essential fear

1

that new thoughts introduced to their peoples will diminish control over their interests (political and/or religious) seems to dominate such an attitude. A sensitive framework of cultural values was suddenly opposed by radical change as institutions of higher learning revealed the errors of the past and degraded a mysticism which served a few to rule over the many. Since radical change provides emotional upheaval, in most cases depriving the masses of the time they need to adapt to a new situation, the subsequent condition of incapability to adapt will cause confusion and panic. **Rapid change carries along with it the danger of conflict since human emotions react abruptly when time and change are being condensed.**

Evolution has, over time, created living space for certain peoples on this earth. China, therefore, was to be of the Chinese for the Chinese as Greece was distinctly Greek and Africa distinctly for the Africans. Africa, more modern by concept already in antiquity, had its northern part inhabited by races which looked and acted differently than elsewhere. The modern world, that is to say North America, has, however, made the first gigantic step forward into a new age where man is not being tied any longer to his traditional regions but where the globe is being shared in the concept of free movement and the ideal of liberty for all. Here civilization, not an invention of nature but rather a manmade concept, has begun to finally blossom after severe struggle and suffering had its first centuries lost to the tribulations from clashes of cultures and dreams. The war which liberated mankind from slavery proved to be the most costly war which was ever fought by the American people: brother slaying brother to free those who had been brought

2

here against their own will. This occurred when British control governed the affairs of a region which was subsequently taken over to begin a new era, that of the United States of America. The northern peoples of the Union were outraged over the maintenance of racial abuse, resulting in a cruel war: one which produced the highest loss of human life of all the wars the United States of America would ever find themselves involved in. It was now up to the remaining former slaves to find a place in society: a task which was unachievable since tradition and status forbade assimilation. Much talk and little science were being applied in order to introduce these different looking people to each other's realm so they eventually could learn that, in fact, no true difference existed. Blood transfusions proved that the same species man, in fact, was at hand, discrediting infamous reports which proclaimed otherwise. Unfortunately, the very same institution which struggled to free the slaves was now dividing them into secondary groups. The ignorant, antiquated belief had it that dark was evil: the night offers darkness, uncertainty. Dark clouds hold thunder. Dark was the symbol for being unclean, shady and not trustworthy.. and so on. Here, in truth, lay the cultural affliction with which the new citizens were still handicapped: a leftover from antiquity which offered no redeeming features for any new order. As man, the individual as well as his group, struggled and emerged a new order seemed to evolve despite the many inherent problems which form a part of man's continuous struggle anywhere on this globe. Since many of these problems remain a dilemma stemming more from his innermost emotions, man has to be schooled to learn much more about himself; that is, the individual should be taught as to how he

3

functions and why he functions in the fashion in which it appears that he does.

The global problems are now being unloaded onto each and every modern human being. To be informed and to remain informed is something which is being expected and essential in order to be able to remain a part of the achieving world. Here, through the media, the printed word or the spoken one will reach millions of minds and, therefore, this same media should ensure that it is worthy of such an immense responsibility. Yet, more and more does it appear that the media serves itself firstly, since messages are being sent with the need to create revenues or are tied into the effort of earning income. In order to sell their information with secured profits, intense emotional input is being delivered to each and every human being. It is not the concern of the media as to whether the individual can cope with the very involved dispatches (a factual emotional breaking point cannot be readily proven), primarily because this attitude of business was a creation of evolution and not planned in the outset. Information, which comes packaged across the television screen, has been in most instances already edited for a specific use and purpose, since the main driving force propelling the results (even from newscasts) remains the source of income, the advertiser behind all such performances. Therefore, news will be dramatized, directed and edited to achieve a certain end, not serving the native source, the actual event, but all that which can be derived from that event. Since a social intercourse with the screen and its reporters is impossible, each and every individual begins to store the events and their impacts which are being broadcast to us until one can relate this information to others or sort such information out within one's own mind. The amount of information which enters our minds and bodies is burdened with emotional properties of a very wide range and must therefore be controlled by the human mind. If it is analyzed, understood and put to rest in the memory, it will serve us at a later time for numerous reasons and occasions. However, if such information is piled up, if new personal emotional input enters without end and if the demand load upon the conscious and subconscious mind remains unbalanced,  with no vent or recourse  being offered, the human mind begins to suffer. Much information is being measured and compared regarding the conscience (morals) each individual holds within himself. Such overload begins to evoke a certain type of stress, differing in kind from other such inputs which overload the human mind. The media, in their efforts to inform, do so regardless as to the capability of the individual tolerances for message overload. As a matter of fact dramatic news, as far as selling is concerned, is considered *great* news, since the people become literally tied to the screen! Desert Storm, the last war, took place within the living room and brought great earnings and stunning results as every human being wanted to back the troops and needed the verification of success. (The engagement of warfare in itself planted upon the screen action, adventure! What would occur when the action changes in favour of the enemy, the war being lost blow by blow? Would the general public have enough mental resource to endure after a disastrous campaign? Remember! Many victorious conflicts first showed losses; lost battles before the side in favour finally moved firmly toward victory!) However, the media rarely carries pleasant news. Each and every newscast, on a daily basis, reveals the troubles and hurts of mankind in packaged form, mostly hard hitting. Since every human being reacts to overload differently, do some persons begin to show signs of depression, a slowing down in activity; while for others the adaptive impulse within will make them seek out new interests. In any case, news overload coupled with other daily survival demands on the citizen begin to promote action of some sort. It is the desire of most healthy and stable minds to solve problems, to speak and talk in order to relate to sources of discomfort, anguish or torment. If this cannot be done, disorder begins to set in. It is true that a well adjusted person might be able to turn his mind off, shout or turn the set off; nonetheless, an ever-increasing number of people begin to involve themselves with their emotions, at times suffering enough to seek out the assistance of a physician. They feel that something has changed within them. Knowing that things are no longer as simple as they were years or even months ago, some begin to inquire of the right source. Unfortunately, many "self-help" attempts end up channeling other persons over to drug and alcohol use; a road which is easy to enter and almost always, without exception, impossible to leave.

Having mentioned before that the powerful human emotions direct us much easier toward conflict than we think, reason, the capability to reason, in most instances will be counteracted upon by this emotional interference: nature forcing itself upon the human mind before reason, civilization does. However, *if properly trained*, the innate survival instinct of man can be used to overcome this phenomenon. This mainly occurs when a certain **correct action** is commenced to secure a situation, especially one wherein there is a threat to life and belongings. For example: A pilot, flying a twin

First Stage

*Emotion*

TRAINING

Second Stage

**Reason**

7

engine aircraft is trained beforehand to follow a precise regimen in the event that one of his two engines fails. In the first hours of such training, it is the instructor who simulates an emergency by reducing the revolutions of one of these two engines considerably, giving the student the belief that that particular engine has failed. This will make itself very quickly known since the well running opposite engine begins to exert its power by pulling the aircraft into a circle. Obviously, from the moment one motor fails, the pull will now be seriously one-sided: a deadly encounter for anyone being caught unaware and who has never before been conditioned, *trained*, to overcome such an emergency situation. During the first attempts at training for such an event most students panic. Their emotions are suddenly burdened with so much fear that orderly thinking becomes almost impossible, depriving them of a precise, sequential counteraction. **Only the correct reaction, not just any reaction, will remedy the situation**. If a student is being trained with care and gradually introduced to this condition, he will eventually master the event in such a way that it does not matter whether it occurs with his knowledge or happens as a true emergency at any given moment in time. **The subconscious mind will then not bother with any emotional interference. It has now become possible to ascertain reason through training, not allowing any other emotional thought to interfere with such learning, crystallizing knowledge through conditioning, arriving at the understanding of certain human inadequacies and seeking out possibilities to change matters toward one's advantage.**

However, this simplification can mislead. Modern motivators are in business to teach us how to succeed. A streamlined approach is created to secure results. Results in turn relate to money and success: first, for the inventor and only secondly, then, for the student, the consumer. Having the back streets laden with inactive peoples this seems to be, if one can believe the motivator, the panacea for modern day failure. Rapid group motivation and mind conditioning are, of course, a thriving enterprise but in general do not produce the results which were advertised and thus had become acclaimed procedures, abdicating the gloom and doom atmosphere with which the unlearned and unskilled populations are being confronted. An entire industry has thus arrived overnight and private colleges have expanded their curriculum promoting the idea of "simplified success." The universities, on the other hand, have begun to introduce more complicated methods of teaching: new math!!.... and also new techniques for spelling skills, though little advance has been made in the general standards of education. The pioneering attitude of bygone days (**first things first**) was being scoffed at while an ever increasing number of paper scholars began to prove that they were existing rightfully; thus complicating simple procedures, introducing psychological trickery, compounding such complications thereby inviting new specialists from the halls of learning onto the stage of public achievement. **Common sense** knowledge was not in demand any longer since the universities do not issue degrees for such pragmatic skills. Governments began to interfere with the system of learning: the learned ones securing their markets by means of organizing themselves within the government structure. The much feared "Red Tape" syndrome began to permeate our society in the end severing the links provided to seek out professional advice,

9

fearing double talk and profiteering, thus hurting the dedicated professional who wishes to assist his fellowman. Modern man is being catapulted into a quagmire of problems which derive from a society which has begun to complicate its affairs in such a way that it becomes impossible to sustain clarity of mind, thought, and to direct one's efforts accordingly. As much as the "Thousand points of Light" are a welcome idea, that of putting initiative into the hands of the people instead of relying only on the governments for sole action, much more emphasis should be placed on the simple fact that the individual must learn to understand that correct self-help, that re-direction of one's activities, can create lasting results far superior to other methods known if it stems from learned sources.

Observation has been made (and scientifically the recordings evaluated) that whenever an excellent motivator and teacher had the opportunity to address a group of people a certain type of success was definitely attainable. From a crowd of a hundred persons about five would begin to plan, learn and redirect their lives in accordance with the program they attended. These are the persons who provide the testimonials in pre-recorded performances in order to persuade many people to think and re-direct their ways. Unfortunately, the primary motivator is usually using and appealing to greed, the urge for wealth, in order to propel his own success. In an industrial environment, this type of motivator will perform for a large amount of money, only too willing to stir up the mass of listeners. Everyone's attention is being maintained by means of a **mind bending** concept, the presence of a large crowd providing the emotional stability, security and strong feeling that truth has been delivered only to learn two weeks later that most of the listeners are back in their "old seats" so to speak, while the proportion of the rate of success (the five persons in a hundred) prevailed: meaning that about 95 persons will have to admit to themselves that things did not work out for them as was promised to them. Psychologists agree, in general, that these five persons would have eventually succeeded without intensive motivation in any case. They were of the dormant, positive type. Negative persons rarely succeed for any length of time and, as observed here, as soon as the motivating force declines they will return to their natural way, the negative cycle to which they had adapted. The problems of these persons are never examined nor are they in a hopeful situation from the point of conduct of the motivator. Since the person motivating does a great service to society, at least freeing the five individuals from their demise of inaction within the hundred who will continue to accept their lot, do we see that remuneration derives from the fact that it is possible to succeed. Here we return to the well prepared "Hollywood Style" of performance in which converts tell all. Yet, a great injustice is being done to all the others who now, suddenly, are being confronted with the fact that they actually did not "have it", resigning themselves to a lasting acceptance of fate: one which is now more endowed with failure than ever before. A few, just a very few individuals, will suffer severely from what they now perceive to be a setback, seeing failure in themselves which in fact really was not their fault.

The structural, emotional make-up to succeed does not lie in the finding of wealth but in the happiness which comes from the realization to act firstly; and secondly in the awareness of the discovery of one's potential whatever that potential might be.

Monetary return remains a by-product of the previous only, comparing it to luck, which one cannot obtain in a store as a ready-made item. Luck remains a by-product of something, of at least a try or attempt at something. Luck for the most part is not something one could rely upon for any great length of time unless one can create the conditions where luck ceases to remain chance and is converted into success.

Crass greed, the promise of great wealth, remains for commercial motivators the most practical tool in order to gain attention for their lectures. Yet, of the five persons who in fact succeed being so motivated three will, in time, also flounder.

**Lasting success** consists of specific ingredients and demands many things of which greed and the drive for wealth and notoriety are most unreliable companions. You see, money, notoriety, and whatever else attaches itself to this, are also a by-product, not so much of success (it first has to set in, it has to principally function before it can do something for us), but of **the desire to do something well**, something one likes to do and is good at doing (or becomes good at doing while being involved). Any enterprise can only hope to continue to function if one understands the one and only thing which remains of importance to it: people, the human being is who we have to interact with. Any one person can start almost any business, this does not constitute a problem; however, *can they endure* and most of all *can they flourish and expand*? Do they understand that **people**, you and I, make their business what it becomes? After all: it is nothing at the outset other than an intent to engage in offering either merchandise or a service. Most business persons who are driven by greed, seeing the customer as the person through whom they wish to enrich themselves, are doomed to never find a lasting success: it will but only brush their shoulder. It is alike the soul who wished to catch a butterfly, working so hard to obtain it, running after it with great effort, yet failing. But when, on another day, this person sat down and minded his affairs the butterfly came, so goes the story, and sat softly on his shoulder.

In retrospect: if then, as we have previously discussed, approximately five persons from any chosen crowd of a hundred can be made to succeed, we begin to ask the question as to why 95 of the present did not? We are being told that nothing succeeds like success does: a proverbial cliche which is all too often repeated and less often understood. What then are the true pre-requisites in order to understand this something, this positive force, this drive or desire which makes people perform wonders? Well, firstly, a certain honesty is required in order to even begin to comprehend this affair in which we wish to be engaged.

I:      There are no miracles which can be found, unearthed or invented which offer any one human being a guarantee to achieve success at anything.

II:     If claims of success are being advertised, the advertisement will concern itself with people who will admit that they have succeeded. If five or even ten or twenty out of a crowd of a hundred persons have begun to succeed, this still leaves a powerful amount of eighty such persons stranded: a very negative amount if one wishes to promote results.

        Remember: you will hear of the ones who have made it and you, yourself, will want to believe that the majority of all the people being addressed have done so.   THIS IS SIMPLY NOT THE CASE. Granted, if indeed ten or even twenty people from a large crowd can be made to change their ways, they might appear to succeed at first but upon second observation, time will have suddenly absorbed their energy into nothing. They have simply faded away into oblivion, the woodwork: they have gone with the wind and ducked under away from friends and relations in order to avoid the inevitable embarrassment. The "big" attitude will have changed to a far lesser one, hiding away from the questions to avoid the answers which rarely can be given. Failure itself is also a by-

14

product: one which belongs more prevalently to success since failure cannot produce its own demise, it already entails dereliction.

III:     Success, in itself, is only of value if it can be made to last and it will only last if we have no false illusion pertaining to its chemistry. It is here and here alone where it becomes consequential to understand that lasting success will have to come from a strength which must reside inside of the individual, and, if it is not there it cannot be readily instilled with a formula which guarantees that it would remain of a long duration. The persuasive powers of a motivator might have injected some impetus into his pupil, making such a person believe that it was he, himself, who acted alone but quickly would he learn that he was being carried by the strength of someone else. When the flame extinguished, when the words of persuasion ended, nothing was capable of keeping the flame going. Most people begin now to experience deep-seated disappointment and disbelief: the same feelings if not worse from which they just believed they had been saved and herein lies the greatest danger.

# BUT I WAS TOLD ...

But I was told to aim and strike
and rid my soul of all it knows,
to lean against or pull to fight
and change my method as it goes.

The goal so high, so empty was the aim,
that all my friends forgot my face
and the success was one which never came:
the spot I held a lonesome place.

The talkmen left, the curtain fell,
their promises could not fulfill
when one turns heaven into hell
by selling angels with the till.

# Chapter II

◆

# The Foundation

"In nothing does man come closer to
God than in doing good to other men."

The liberation of the human spirit has directed the mind toward its own inventions creating, in time, a new outlook upon the world in which one lives. Total and instant communication, the prompt storing of data, as well as the instantaneous ability to recall such information has allowed for an insight into anything and all the mind confronts, creating an enormous superstructure of information upon which all knowledge is being built. The human mind is expected to function alike a machine, ready to accept a never ending amount of new material. It is not only required that the newly trained human being (the child) learn of all the past inventions and intellectual discoveries mankind accumulated but that this being should also attempt to catch up with the onslaught of new scientific discoveries by which our century is being propelled into the next one to come.

Though a machine can serve man with a given productive capability for an indefinite time period it will, sooner or later, arrive at a point of failure. Parts will wear out, chemicals will alter their composition as printed circuits begin to fail thus losing their functions. Whenever this occurs, all is being dropped back into the lap of the human being who remains somewhere behind this gigantic, structured support system.

It is true that the human mind has immense capabilities to store and recall learned information; in fact, digesting and absorbing all the knowledge man has accumulated over his nine thousand years of recorded history and much more, coping even with the speculation of the creation of his own and all other known species in the universe, mapping and compiling the structure of the universe itself, researching visible and invisible matter, solving concrete as well as abstract problems. Storming thus ahead into the future, he has begun to divide and share this massive amount of information, to specialize by choosing different branches of knowledge and skills and to perfect them, each to his own, never losing touch with the rest of his kind who share into this great adventure of progress.

Thus, modern man has placed his mind directly into the middle of the universe, refusing to accept the scintillating stars as being mere poetic sparkling diamonds in the eternally frozen cosmos. He has observed, measured and compared and knows of the opposites. The eternally cold gives way to the super hot atomic bursts within such stars. While his mind comprehends the abstract in its numbers of infinity does he shudder if such information has to be absorbed by his emotional make-up. The present, relentlessly progressing modern world relies upon the mind of man to serve it. It expects his mind to behave alike the machines which are a reflection of his mind but are not a substance of its living organism. While all his machines can be replaced, repaired or even rebuilt, can his mind however not undergo such total restructuring as easily

18

as it can be done with a machine, by replacing defective parts with new ones. The mind, created by evolutionary forces, is integrated into the entire biochemical and physical concept of the being, and in fact is resting in part on a foundation blending both the emotional and spiritual with the concrete physical.

The human mind exposed to the process of learning is capable of dealing with an immense volume of information, astounding as it appears; but remains, quite remarkably so, very adept at processing and evaluating this data. The mind has, in most cases, a neutral, unemotional basis if it is involved in the compiling of external, non-humanly related information. The acts of reading, painting, adding or subtracting, listening to a teacher or searching for answers involve each individual in a different way but do not involve his innermost feelings in these processes unless human inadequacies are being introduced or be it that the process in itself falters; thus introducing negative human responses.

Our mind, in essence, seems to endure many influences which stimulate and direct it. With the coming of age of medicine's latest accepted branch of science, psychology, man's mind has been observed more closely and, thus, is better understood than ever before. However, specialization, the process which groups and isolates sections of scientific information for the purpose of use and instruction, keeps each branch of science, such as medicine, within the realm of its instructive evolution. The general practice of medicine still holds the center isle of all the related arts and sciences with its rapidly expanding special branches of knowledge from immunologic discoveries to the new nuclear methods of cell research, to computer analyzed three dimensional pictures, ending

19

really nowhere but in the micro filing systems of massive electronic storage banks, the knowledge being retrievable here at any time for all those who need to use that information in order to keep abreast with these many levels of learning. Such information storage centers will, in the future to come, afford some relief to the individual human being, allowing data exchange on a very wide spectrum involving all branches of science for better and more efficient integration.

It was not long ago when human behavior was believed to entail a mainly genetic, inherited phenomenon and the mind was not really understood in its conceptual function. Neurology, the study of nerves and nerve cells, the transmission of impulses of motion, pain, direction and orientational capabilities of the human mind with its interacting electro-chemical as well as biological consequences, became another specialty in the vast empire of such ever expanding knowledge. Parapsychology has, as of late, attracted many scientists as well as witch doctors alike. As a matter of fact, this free flow of information amidst a free enterprise system has introduced pseudo healers and quick cure merchants in great abundance with an astonishing effrontery to boast of their quackery.

The fifteenth century produced quacks in great abundance for many reasons. Firstly, the great leap forward, the Age of Reason, the Renaissance was about to begin alike the phoenix who climbed out of the ashes - not the ashes of a dying fire but the ashes of ignorance. Superstition was soon to be overcome by reason, that ever dormant spark within those searching minds: minds of a great spiritual as well as intellectual reformation. The ignorant masses themselves participated in this "sturm und drang" period (Goethe) throughout the Western world. The stranglehold of the dominating churches which had held the minds of their contemporary scientists captive was being broken until even the churches succumbed to a more freer investigation of their surrounding world.

However, the ongoing struggle of inquiry into mind and matter still kept certain social forces in disarray until modern schooling methods and free societies introduced the separation of church and state. This occurrence, however, also began to lessen the spiritual drive behind those great human minds: minds which had a deep appreciation for God and church, despite their struggle with that formidable institution to acquire sufficient freedom for their own minds in order to rescue man from established ignorance. As freedom became a legal entity and when the state began to guarantee rights for all no matter what, a basic preamble of human conduct was also being forfeited. While this event was important and could not have been achieved otherwise, legislating the rights of all thus securing them without that discrimination could occur, the state failed to sustain its leadership in concept; since the awarded rights were not necessarily connected to any reciprocities by the citizen. It was not essential to remain deserving of such given rights. Referring to the state as such, it is here understood that a democratically organized state is being chosen; since any other type of politically organized structure fails to offer anything in order to even begin to find a comparison.

The democratically organized state had to evolve in such a way: the state leading in trust, offering rights firstly in the hope that the grateful citizen would repay it by leading a life from which the state (that is the rest of society) would benefit. Rome, in its days of splendor, created such a society in part. However, its interests grew far past its borders, where its legions defended the structural state in far lands, losing the spiritual intent of their given legislation, teaching the citizen over time how to make a living off the legal provisions the state offered too freely.

Juvenal (60 - 140 AD) describes his friend's reason as to why he was leaving the city of Rome:

> *"Since there is no place for honest pursuits, no profit can be got by honest toil - my fortune is less today than it was yesterday. What shall I do at Rome? I cannot lie: if a book is bad, I cannot praise it and beg a copy. I know not the motions of the stars. I neither will nor can promise a man to secure a father's death. I never inspected the entrails of a toad: no one shall be a thief by my cooperation. Who, nowadays, is beloved except the confidant of crime?"*

Much friction of human emotions through circumstance derives from the spreading of disorder (especially in legal matters). All that which was started with great thought centuries ago is systematically being eroded. The intent of legislation which was created at the outset was not truly put into writing and assumed to be a definite understanding based upon the moral structure of that time. All thoughts and ideas, ideals as well, have since faced a rapidly progressing society which is receiving its legal protection from the inspired works of their noble leaders of bygone days. If one recalls the exalted words of the constitution, now, as they present themselves, one can sense the dominant moral force of that time. The underlying moral code, deriving from the Holy Script, was, in thought of great fairness, never mentioned; as if to not injure the minority of other, diverse, beliefs.

It is because of these previously shown involvements that the human mind is being engaged in attempting to maintain a general direction of responsibility to a code of moral and ethical conduct. However, man's emotions are much more involved in his struggle to survive than ever before: intimidated just by the mere number of equally trained individuals growing into the hundreds of millions of human beings (or only but a select few) with whom he now has to compete in order to survive in a world in which a certain expected standard of living is being awarded only to the ones who remain successful in that struggle. Those who are unaware or unable to perform in this setting are left behind.

A free society permits its citizens to organize themselves for any cause, idea or aim. It is primarily here where the struggle between good and evil is being waged: it is the political arena, the one which is being created by a group of capable citizens and forfeited by the less capable type.

**"In nothing does man come closer to God than in doing good to other men."**

Such proverbial lines can be found on the time bleached walls of the ancient temples; but, observing rather closely and understanding the building and eroding forces only time carries along with itself, it became clear that, foremost, modern man derives goodness from that which benefits him. Unfortunately, the emphasis of the teachings in the temples and churches toward goodness have themselves eroded in time and are being directed by rather pragmatic visions, forwarded as progress, success and other new utopian visions of well-being. Of course, there is such a state of affairs as success and failure and it remains of the utmost of importance that these concepts are being understood for their valuable relations to human nature. Thus, to motivate the citizen by inducing greed, one will succeed swiftly, securing quick response as the "human reward system" can at once identify with such aims. Income, business derives benefit promptly from this approach as the motivated parties pay their dues for the *secrets* which have been departed to them by the motivator. However, these so-called secrets are rather superficially structured, organized, having the generating drive which must come from the individual in mind. Since the motivator replaces the individual in his session, knowing full well that he will have to withdraw from his function as soon as the session ends, he instills the powerful impulse of greed, hoping that this force will continue to propel the motivated party onward. This, of course, is not so and aside from this observation many unwelcome and dangerous aspects are being propagated in such a paltry attempt as society will have to deal with the fallout, the failure, when these created dreams come to an unwelcome end. This will inevitably occur as soon as the power of the motivation begins to lessen, each individual assuming their own, previously held natural state of behavior: the state of mind in which they were originally found by the forces which began to remove them from that state for but a few hours, days or weeks. You see, not every human being progresses in a rational manner: something which is of no real concern to the group who engages in the sessions as long as they can prove that *some* people derive "great benefit" from their teachings. Duration or qualification is not being addressed for obvious reasons: it would impose concrete limitations on the entire program. The failures and disasters resulting from these endeavors are never discussed.

If a choice can be made between health and poverty or sickness and wealth, the rational individual would quickly choose to prefer wealth and health! The human mind is tied to human emotions and most of us are not equally as well equipped to tolerate failure as we are naturally equipped to afford success. It is here where much harm is being done to a vast group of citizens, some even counteracting their beliefs and conscience.

**Remember: when you override your conscience you are laying the groundwork for an emotional disaster.**

# Chapter III

♦

# Strength from where?

"...some functions of the mind are
paralleled to evolution and are deeply
rooted.."

The first mind is a part of the second mind, both having a common origin, being of each other. In fact, there is in truth no second mind but rather a first, a mind only, occurring in two or more stages....the first stage being the programming stage, the second being the storing type only. The first stage's most powerful programming occurs from emotional experiences.

It is said that nothing succeeds like success and that nothing seems to fail like failure; apparently the **likes**, here explained as being occurrences of the same kind, seem to enforce each other in either direction of the scale. Indeed, no one would be seriously concerned if a person would continue to succeed without ever failing. On the other hand, is it a quite serious matter if one keeps on continuously failing in most of the things one attempts to achieve.

One could almost assume that the first type of person, who appears to succeed without ever failing, lives from a unique strength which rests somewhere deep inside of him as if nature has bestowed such individuals with a certain gift, a special talent, so to speak. Friends, parents and neighbors are convinced that anything that one particular person touches will turn to gold. Since this seems to be an exaggeration, nevertheless: each and every human being starts on the same road to life, some roads being better paved than others, of course, in order to make their way. How then is it that some human beings struggle much harder than others, only to find out that they are succeeding even less today than they have on the previous day? If they compare themselves with the person who, supposedly, possesses the "golden touch", they eventually begin to lose hope and fall into utter despair. Scientists have learned that the human mind functions within a framework of varying emotions, each type exerting a distinct authority over the subsequent emotional state it creates. In short, your mind is affected by positive or negative influences in distinct and almost certain ways. All human beings might have been created equal but they are *uniquely* different in their individual "make-up", leaving a very personal, distinct mark on the emotional structure of each and every human being. If this "make-up", this something, could be understood, we could be privy to some *insight* into our actions and, in many cases, induce change for the better, wherever this is warranted.

A few moments ago, we discussed the fact that all people are supposedly of equal creation yet are still somewhere very different from each other. One could now begin to talk of the inherited parts, the genetic material, by which one mind may function in a very distinct and different way from the next. One could introduce other relevant observations into this discussion, at once beginning to diffuse this examination before it really is allowed to seek out a general direction, exploding thus into nothingness. By allowing a gradual approach, one can slowly develop a measured concept and look upon the subject matter of man and mind less pointedly, rather more universally, not dictating knowledge but creating a mosaic of observances which must then be channeled and placed in a rational order, allowing the reader to comprehend this material at his leisure, putting it together in accordance with his or her ability.

If, for the sake of this discussion, we set aside disorders and illnesses of the mind, we would find that in many cases little difference in all of our behavior toward success or failure exists other than the fact that our minds have undergone varying experiences, either growing up, developing upwards, in an uplifting way (a much needed emotional frame of mind) toward success or downward, aiming toward failure. In dealing with the human mind, one cannot truly produce a blueprint for success or failure within the structured mind but one can learn to understand the forces, the future shaping forces, by which our minds function. **Healthy emotions are essential in order to cultivate constructive attitudes toward life.** Often though, do many people suffer from lack of courage, a demise which lies buried somewhere deep within us, influencing our outlook, our attitudes, diminishing our positive, our creative forces. Having learned that a positive outlook does affect our lives for the better, do many people marshal their senses in order to succeed. They even go into business for themselves. Yet, when the first signs of success ebb, so does their positive energy and subsequently they fail... As much as courage is a welcome source of mental energy, the entire chemistry upon which success depends was never present from the start and, in fact, not understood altogether.

Schooled motivators give seminars and make presentations, apply sound and pictures to present proof of high earnings before an enthusiastic crowd; however, as soon as they depart only but a few will have made the transition, remain motivated and continue to do so. The reason is simply that these few individuals would have succeeded anyway needing only an example, a talking to, as this colloquialism best describes it, in order to get going. Some channeling of their minds and a direction as to where to get the information, some guidance they felt was all they needed. The rest they would discover as they went on to explore the newly found freedom success so readily seemed to provide in the offing. As previously mentioned, out of a crowd of a hundred people being so motivated only one or two such persons are capable of sustaining their success. The remainder of the crowd ends up in frustration, often being penniless after having spent most of their hard earned savings on the seminar which was to mark a new beginning; yet was, invisibly so, bestowed with failure from the start. The main drive behind any motivation toward success lies in the offering of an easy life, unlimited earnings, etc. Many real estate/investment companies travel and offer proof of large earnings, telling us what to do and how to operate; yet, again, most of the people attending are quickly overcome by failure and despair.

Since greed, earnings, and the good life are promised, do they provide a most powerful motivating force to each and every living human being. However, this type of approach can literally destroy many unsuspecting people. After all: who would not like to earn a high profit, a lasting income, for the rest of one's earthly days? The salesperson begins to talk of the scheme by which it is possible to *make* a lot of money, providing that the underlying structure delivered by the lecturer is also well understood by the crowd. To begin with: a psychological error is being proffered here, since money may not be made by anyone legally unless he or she is working for the mint. The mint makes money: the rest of the people have to go to work and earn it! The person who now begins to enter the big world of the entrepreneur will soon find this out for himself and the easy making of income quickly disappears as the harsh world of tomorrow begins to present itself. In order to really understand the actual precise steps toward betterment one has to know something about his very own person. Honesty regarding certain shortcomings is essential in order to even begin to set out on the road toward betterment. You see, the successful person has most of the ingredients within himself already and works well with them, either knowingly or by intuition. At times, a good personality and honest service will do a great deal if one engages in a business venture. Sadly enough most persons do not really know what it is they are trying to achieve prior to their being involved in an enterprise other than that their thoughts are being propelled by the idea of huge earnings and large windfall profits. It appears that they, in fact, do not really care, as long as they can achieve such a goal, a dream as they are told, which will come true as long as they continue to strongly believe in it; but so, literally spoken, do millions of other people as well! Therefore, it is fair to assume that only the best equipped will remain in business and the rest will have to learn from experience. To remain in business alludes here simply to all the tasks life in itself offers and may, from time to time,

31

provide. Success may begin or end if opportunities are being missed on a continual basis.

The Neo Ch'an philosophy concurs with modern science, meaning that certain prerequisites have to be present within any one human being before she or he can truly become successful, achieving the chemistry within us necessary to endorse lasting results. Being the world leader of the Neo Ch'an concepts, We remain, however, opposed to the concept of motivating crowds, trying to propel greed into success: an enterprise which may appear workable in general but will in most cases fail to serve the individual or the state, barring but a few fortunate souls who had the right "make-up" somewhere already within themselves. However, in the Neo Ch'an concept we believe that this spark, this power which we refer to as the **Shen Ch'i,** exemplifies the driving force within all of us being of sound mind and body.

Leaving the mysticism behind, which has wasted away precious centuries in alchemistic attempts to produce science where none existed, the Neo Ch'an concept attempts not to denounce the achievements of the ancients but rather to highlight their strength and perseverance. The great trial and error method with which the ancients worked served them well enough until their civilization was confronted by the Greek concepts: the Western World arriving at the theory that was even able to prove the abstract by means of science, deduction becoming the driving force behind great minds and greater achievements, saving centuries of wasteful verification. Being inspired by modern thought and progressively reforming ancient concepts, the Neo Ch'an philosophy does only lean on some of the past Buddhist beliefs whenever the human soul is being

32

addressed. It would be fair to say that we see in this direction of thought a philosophical attempt to better the world by way of attitude than by religious prompting. Thought, however, demands proper guidance and cannot be tolerated without the understanding of scientific values: science being that force which created the word "Neo", Latin for the word new. Ch'an thoughts were introduced sometime ago but fell by the wayside, fearing modern thought and ideas, hovering with the old, scared to clear the dust of the remaining works of the ancients. It is fair to assume, giving China the pretext that history had excluded them from a modernization of thought, that no such excuse should continue to linger on in time. Freedom of thought was not as readily tolerated by the emperors of that ancient civilization and unfortunately the modern day revolution has again cut the great cord of communication by which human enquiry seems to flourish best. Amidst these observations is it apparent then that the problem of modern day man exists within his very own realm, every region fostering certain conditions by which man has to abide in order to succeed; fortunately, "If you come to Athens you do as the Athenians do" does not apply in our free and much blessed nation. In order to elucidate the problems which surround man's success and failure, our concept for achieving lasting results as successful human beings requires that a **code of attitudes** be understood before any further details can be discussed pertaining to this most desired enterprise, a code of attitudes pertaining to what success and failure should constitute in our lives in order to afford a successful future the right way.

The Neo Ch'an concept sees its own exercise, which is stemming from the Ch'i Hu Temple, as a pre-condition toward the leading of a successful life. Of course any exercise, reasonable exercise, can become a pre-condition toward such aim. Life is motion and only good movement will secure all that which fundamentally arrives at a good personal standard of health. (Through thousands of years man had to survive by staying in constant motion: he had to hunt in order to feed himself, chasing the ever elusive game with all his vigor.) Individuals do differ pertaining to their own health requirements and it is up to each person to remain informed as to which exercise is deemed to be worthwhile or not for one's very own physique or state of health. A certain frame of mind as well seems to be even more essential before anything else should be considered. Such frame of mind will interact with exercise in a unique but natural way. Experience has shown that mind and body work best together if a continuous interaction between the two can be secured. A reasonable amount of exercise therefore will benefit the human mind greatly. Exercise stimulates the brain activity and generates a healthy bio-chemistry within the brain cells, stemming from an increased blood flow to a heightened electrochemical exchange in the brain. As a matter of fact, the ancients learned that monks who felt depressed and lacked incentive would change their attitudes toward activity quickly and noticeably whenever they engaged in the movements of their art. Modern science has now isolated a type of biochemical substance in the brain which is responsible, in part that is, for an emotional uplift, becoming a motoring device for desire and participation: in short, removing the normal downward trend from the emotions of the individual. One speaks here of the normal individual who is lacking incentive because of mild depression. Disorders of the mind

34

which produce depression will not necessarily be touched by this phenomenon: activity, exercise will not undo a disorder which might have a deeply rooted cause within the psyche of an individual.

This philosophical precept, this recognition of mind-body unity, was by no means novel to the ancient Chinese but created the world which was Greek, that type of antiquity which equaled the Chinese drive for knowledge but would not waste entire centuries as did the Chinese before they were able to put much of their discoveries within a proper, that is scientific, frame of observation. Of course, many of the claims which stemmed from religious practices remained nebulous in meaning and substance when the leaders learned that mysticism lends itself best to claiming powers before the ignorant: powers the ignorant respected but which were not really owned. Henceforth, the observation that super human forces were at play (that is, in observing the demonstrations of a yogi, depriving his body for some length of time of the bare essentials, either oxygen, water, etc.) made a lasting impact on such minds but were in fact false; since the yogi, a human being, gave the performance, it had to be of a living being, unless the human being was to be replaced by the posture of a yogi, one offering a conflict, a contradiction to the other. The ancient Chinese learned soon that anyone, not only a yogi, could do likewise, providing he, or she, had the desire to learn and work in order to achieve results in kind. The Chi Hu masters referred to these performers as charlatans, mendicants, since many of the performances of these people made little sense. Nothing was to be gained, in the mind of the observing masters, when the effort did not relate to practical use: a man crawling into a tiny box and remaining there for sometime made no sense! When health, longevity and wisdom remained absent even less interest could be commanded by these achievements. They remained simply exercises which were clad in contortions injurious to the average person. Mysticism has always exerted a magical power upon the minds of living man. The feats of the yogis were rather observed on the spur of the moment; and thus, appeared to relate to fact. The many performers who died in failed experiments made little impact upon the ignorant; but, whenever they succeeded in their folly much was reported and spoken and even embellished. Henceforth, there still are a large circulation of Oriental mystical skills being peddled by latecomers to this continent, presuming to find a like audience in North America. Most people here who would observe a yogi climbing into a tiny box would simply suggest he build the box larger in order to be able to walk right into it, unless some truly worthwhile achievement would result from this type of labor! It would be unfair, however, to discount the efforts of these performers altogether. These exhibitions do point out that man's mind has more powers stored within than we are willing to accept. As this may be the case, **mind training especially shows its success in proportion to time. Some functions of the mind are paralleled to evolution and are deeply rooted**: meaning that they cannot be readily produced in order to combat just any disease, as some persons wish to make us believe. Certain, highly specialized exercises are very demanding and at best become questionable as to their true health value. As a matter of fact, man learned over time that most of these motions could be duplicated by other, less demanding motions capable of being practiced by almost any participant.

36

The Neo Ch'an Buddhist Temple elevated and enhanced Ch'an meditation to become Purposeful Meditation. Its unpretentious methods align themselves best when voluntary participation can be secured. With the reformation of the antiquated trends in Buddhist thought by the Neo Ch'an Temple, an all encompassing new outlook on the world was being unveiled, retaining the word Buddhism in the sense of wisdom, enlightenment, seeking a mature direction. The thought process and the practices of this philosophy are what they are: an outlook on the world as it is and should be, if man's capability to reason could be advanced in such a way. It is not a religious practice in kind but one can become spiritually involved in order to arrive at a religious state of mind where great effort and sacrifice are being extended in order to achieve a beneficial end for all of mankind. This means, here, that not only the mind, the intellectual power of man, is being employed but much moreso his soul becomes involved in order to afford workable human dialogue, offer compassion and understanding without forfeiting moral values: the fiber of which lasting civilizations must be made in order to achieve a peace which remains more durable, thus offering a more lasting state of well-being for the human race. This, in turn, imposes cooperation by the few to the many, trying to solve the dangerous crowding of the planet by our species. The mendacious attitude that life is all, one kind of creation having the sole right to prevail on this planet over all others, must be examined as to retain reason over dogmatic teachings which, in time, will introduce a devastating effect on all of mankind; that is, not to oppose such teachings but to point to the facts and to nature itself and purge most of the man invented

37

religious thoughts so they may no longer have a detrimental impact on life as we see it.

All dogmatic teachings have their own logical surrounding, the purpose for which these teachings have been created. Man, himself, being an imperfect creation, not so much by body but rather by functioning mind, will make it difficult to create a perfect state of affairs on this planet. With the arriving of the 21st century, the industrialized nations will have to learn to respect the environment to a much greater degree than ever before. This does not mean a return into the trees, an all too often forgone conclusion, a betrayal in short of man's achievements; but an honest assessment as to safety, the aspect of health, which is so closely related to our environment. Neither the best car nor the fastest aircraft or largest crop harvested will suffice if ill health is derived from them. In the end, the governments must do all that which has been postponed for too long, delayed and mismanaged: address the problems before nature assumes its part in the regulating process. If the problem of overcrowding cannot be solved then nature in its own way, much less civilized than man, will regulate for him: meaning that the civilized input of man will be taken away from him in opposition to religious doctrines where man is barred from rectifying the massive overcrowding of his planet by his kind, resulting in a shortage of food and employment, pollution, depravation and conflict, infertility, drought, illness, strife and suffering. In short: war, nature's most effective power for regulating the neglected affairs of man, will be invited to begin its work. Such event will cause unheard of suffering and hardship, erasing entire nations from the face of the earth.

Much of the conditions causing such an outrageous overcrowding can be found in the teachings of religious tenets, addressing mankind during the Dark Ages, having control over their minds and struggling to retain such control with all the means which were either affordable or politically astute: more precisely, using the profound understanding of diplomacy, turning the script, if nothing else, against the striving mind of man. Since it is true that the advancing genius of his kind has invited untold problems, it is in the end this same mind, a rational intellect, which alone will be able to deal with his problems. Pinning one religion against the other is, by the way, done rather cunningly and very much so in an indirect fashion using **"mind bending techniques"** on the ignorant and unlearned ones. **The human mind seems to alter its properties when it functions in different surroundings**. If scientific thought is expected to be consistent with the precepts of pure science, one cannot help but observe that this remains only so within the realm of the textbooks. Political science taught in Soviet Russia will differ from that same subject matter if taught in Teheran, Persia. From the day onward where scientific evaluation entered the life of man has he understood to reap from it all that which is beneficial to him, introducing a type of science which, no longer pure in concept and intent, began to serve the ill willed and absurd minded. Democratically orientated nations, in most instances, have retained a much purer, rather untainted version of scientific enquiry: the state preferring to regulate but not restrict the searching minds of its citizens and only doing so when its citizens can point to an abuse in research, proof of such abuse being first discussed before any interference is permitted.

The modern world, as we know it, has had much experience with the past, the bygone centuries. The noted libraries of the world can give an account of the history of our species, tell of the reasons for our failing, our errors and offer remedies for change. Many of our young scientists display more courage and less compliance with what was established, preferring to reveal their findings openly. A primary example of this is the latest achievement of man that of conquering the atom, the ever elusive, invisible something around which even the universe seems to correspond in kind, releasing untold energy to serve mankind. Almost a thousand atomic powered generators were finally constructed and were ready to serve man, his genius triumphant overshadowing his shortcomings, his elated emotions, and along with it his carefree and self-secure outlook pertaining to his invention. As many scientists remain euphoric do others issue serious warnings. Some reactors were built sloppily, some even placed on geographic fault lines: they were built to last forever! Yet, nothing man creates will last that long. The pyramids of Gizeh have eroded more than two meters from the time of their construction. If indeed four thousand years will erode two meters, it is fair to assume that in several hundred million years very little of that structure will be found and along with all that will have gone the great halls of learning, the books and pamphlets of man's genius, the books of the VIP's, the "Who is Who", as well. Nonetheless, as man now functions this cannot be of his concern at this time. Since science has set man's foot into the universe and since he has begun to reflect upon himself, he has learned to deal with problems as they arise and has, indeed, done remarkably well for himself. However, little cooperation is being achieved amongst his kind on a more global scale. Fanatic peoples are being given the tools of destruction in return for monetary gain. China sold nuclear technology to Iran and other countries. The irrational behavior of man seems to have little to do with his genius. Eastern Europe can boast with several dozen nuclear reactors despite the fact that they are on the brink of collapse. Bulgaria sports a complex which groups six such reactors, poorly built, ready to melt down any moment. More than a hundred nuclear fires were being controlled just within the span of one year - radiation permitted to escape, of course! The energy hungry world, industry, has virtually no choice but to keep these power plants functioning; since all other sources of power have been forfeited, being over confident as to what nuclear energy can really accomplish. If the reactors could be built without that funds must be saved, if the safeguards could be put into place with foresight and futuristic responsibility, this energy could perhaps serve man for a long time to come. Yet, the locations of many of these plants are poorly chosen and the problem of the radioactive waste has never been seriously addressed; subsequently, the ground water is being poisoned etc. Thus, a nightmare is being created yet it still has not been made plausible to the general public that such waste will retain its life threatening force for several hundred thousand years. It would take at least a hundred thousand years to clean up the aquifer, the water which comes up crystal clear but has death embodied in its molecular structure for many thousand centuries to come!

The pollution of the atmosphere is not close to being solved as yet nor is the robbery of the rain forest being addressed: the trees which supply the earth with its much needed oxygen. Most of all:

mind pollution, the forces which impair the mind, corrupting it for a distinct purpose, is not even understood, cared for or even researched; yet, it will impact everyone not only the individual adversely, but in fact, in time, will begin to paralyze entire civilizations. It is safe to assume then that future generations will not only have to cope with this problem but are already having to endure the consequences of our illustrious regard for the infallibility of science. It is, therefore, important that good education is being administered to those minds who are serving mankind and to persons who chose the path of science, revering life as it functions, hoping to control all that which can be watched over and guarded from abuse.

**A body nation functions alike the body man.** An infected wound has to be treated, a gangrenous limb removed. Wounds, abuse, crime have to be attended to. Punishment does not match the crime any longer: the gangrenous limb is not being removed, the entire patient left to his demise because deprived minds or elevated minds (over-civilized, effete minds) protect the criminal beyond reason. The death penalty for hideous offenses, gruesome murders, multi killings is termed to be uncivilized, suggesting that the due process of law did not take place at all, which of course is unthinkable in North America. The death penalty is not used to punish everyone who has committed murder. A wide variety of murders are being committed in which human shortcomings resulted in this type of crime and where this crime can be explained, in part, considering the circumstances which led to such a crime. However, it cannot be tolerated any longer that a compassionate society excuses multi murderers, serial killers (one who even ate the remains of his victims after sexually abusing them): in short, any crime which is being planned for gain, crimes where the law is being used to succeed. (Example: a robber can shoot five bank tellers, insuring that his identity remains unknown being aware of the fact that the penalty for one murder remains the same as it is for five). Although civilization is a creation of rational man, does it appear not to be rational, since over time rationality has been expanded, refined to such an extent that it now begins to provide shelter for those who use compassion and tolerance to their advantage. The horrendous costs of keeping sex murderers and the like housed and fed should be passed on to those who wish to provide such services to such criminals. It is acceptable that citizens in a democratic state could arrive at this state of affairs but it is not acceptable that other citizens who are opposed to such irrational thought should pay billions of dollars for those who wish to preach to others that killing is evil but not punishable and is rather an act which needs understanding and forgiveness. Perhaps the state should impose extra taxation on those who wish to afford such laws and let them pay for the maintenance of killers like Manson or Bundy; since the general public is fed up with the free wheeling exploits of groups of people who wish us to pay to care for a satanic being who tries to portray himself to us as having the soul of a human being. It is known that most of them enjoy the act of crime, being master over life and death and especially enjoy the lust and punishment cycle as the victim goes through the final moments of his or her life, in fright and tears often pleading away the most sacred parts of their body and soul to be given some mercy, their God-given life being squashed by some raging madman who

43

planned each and every moment of his adventure to the last detail. Indeed, it appears that his act now has become that of almighty God, since **only acts of God remain unpunished by mortal man**.

The folly of man seems to be embodied in his inability to reason or compromise; henceforth, the centuries are filled with the exploits of the great conflicts by men who altered the borders on this globe as they desired to rule, to become God-like in their vision of these exploits. With the decline of education, the failure to teach tact and manners, knowledge is being generated and propelled without that the soul of man is being cared for. Crowding causes hostility: competition destroys human qualities as in sports where Olympic competing was to be done in such a way as to obey the words of Coubertain that participating, in fact, was more than winning - the desire to win was not subordinated to the drive that raw winning was all, getting the job done any which way.

Our modern world has become very complex and is urged to enjoy competition as a "God sent" answer to productivity. Competition entails very healthy and worthwhile human aspects but begins to cause suffering whenever the human being is pinned against abuse. **Healthy competition differs from the desire to outdo, to humiliate, to surpass any effort put forth by another human being; for, here all efforts are annulled as they are arrived at by forfeiting the rules of human conduct**.

The Neo Ch'an Temple arts are being practiced, therefore, in recognition of such knowledge. Its outlook is elevated over and above that of the ancient concepts using the spiritual values these exercises entail as they free the mind from depression and other such burdens especially that of being incapable to fend for oneself.

44

**The innermost and so little understood ingredient for the achieving of true self-confidence is generated from within by strength and skill, an outward force being extended to the soul enriching it by teaching it to sustain reason and execute compassion while being on the road to become superior in mind and body, not at all over others but very much so over oneself.**

It is in this context that this work is being written and directed. The mind ought to follow the body and both should remain totally integrated with each other, kept in balance so to speak, a natural force which rests deep in the bosom of nature and an act of its very special way of reasoning: **nature does not reason as man does by thought but much moreso by action.** Too much of one thing invites another, a counteracting force, balancing affairs at times in a most uncivil way. War is such an occurrence. Overcrowding can lead to serious conflict. Nations which still are capable of supplying the rest of the world with food cannot be overcrowded and become a haven for those nations which propagate their offspring at the expense of others.

As the twenty-first century approaches on the doorstep of time and as we are progressing still further in the sciences, the struggle to conquer nature, must man address the abuses he affords to his own kind, destroying not only his surrounding, but much moreso his mind: a God-like present issued to him from heaven in order that he may retain his soul, maintaining not only his conscience as well but also the order in his affairs where he may argue and dispute against his genius as well as his downfalls opening an avenue to the future wherein religious opposition does not become a tool to conquer but to unite. **Mind becomes emotion:**

45

**mind in control is emotion in control**. Somewhere in the distant regions of time this could mean that disputes have a chance to be brought into balance. These disputes begin firstly inside of each and every human being before they enter onto the stage of human interaction, either in the realm of the immediate family or are being presented as conflict somewhere else.

These deliberations are here observed at random. However, there are occurrences which affect the human condition in a two-fold manner; influences deriving from outside stimulants and other such forces which are being created inside the human being. Man's global state of affairs, his religious, political and environmental state, his relentless overcrowding of his very own available space, should be considered as an environmental event as well as his state of mind is being directed on a global and national plain. Modern communication links events and conditions of these suggested forces rapidly without necessarily solving them. Religious thought creates overcrowding, the state of which is being created in part by religious thought patterns where birth control, that is family planning, is opposed by the conduct governing doctrine of faith. Therefore, overcrowding is not being addressed in an effective manner, eventually eliminating the very religious groups which are hoping to gain superiority over others through such doctrine. The thoughtless masses, especially the deprived ones, follow an evolutionary drive outproducing the thoughtful ones, the educated ones, who understand that living standards are being governed by certain events. A gradual decline of living standards can be observed as it occurs in every nation on this globe adjusting itself in proportion to the standards of civilized awareness of that

46

particular nation, region etc. In order to address the individual human condition within the individual, must we be aware that the general state of affairs surrounding us will have an effect upon that condition. Stark survival situations will pin the individual against his own kind and create priorities. In many such situations it is not so much the larger family, the nation, which is important to these individuals but much moreso the immediate family. Wherever and whenever survival situations approach in such manner that the individual family must relate to the larger family within such conditions, international conflicts will begin to arrange themselves as an evolutionary, natural event away from the control of thinking, civilized man.

It is here where nature begins to neutralize the efforts of civilization: the struggle mankind began when trying to organize his affairs around the drives of nature. It will be of little benefit to the whole of mankind to succeed in only some places on this globe if they cannot succeed everywhere else in equal measure. A civilized condition in a given nation centers around a balanced economy, production of goods and food being in synchronized levels with a sustained, controlled population growth. Living standards are inadvertently tied to balances of such or equal conditions of affairs. Even if a nation with a vast population could exist for some time, the by-products of a very large population will have to erase gained advantages in compared measure. If such a state would exist, boasting a good living standard because excellent economical management is being adhered to, other less fortunate or less civilized nations will tend to exert enormous pressure on such a successful nation. **A nation does not succeed in its affairs by**

47

**accident equally as much as an individual does not succeed by accident either**. Such nation, such a country, must have arrived at its blessed state of affairs through good government, having little friction within their rows and adhering to the wishes and directions of the thought processes which circulate within that nation.

A general state of tolerance will have to exist within such a nation, since tolerance propels cooperation and thus begins to incorporate a state of well-being amongst its citizens in general. However, tolerance extended to others, coming from different surroundings and from totally different social conditions, can rearrange the state of affairs within such a nation. This, however, only occurs whenever a certain balance is being broken: that is, when too many, when large numbers of foreigners with different attitudes and frames of mind begin to exert influence of a lesser condition than is found entering a new cultural envelope. Since a human's survival ethics can differ vastly if compared to his surrounding, political condition etc., harmony of the soul is being subjected to the events man creates in his own realm. With good management and patience and the will of the newcomers, tolerance should overcome such burden in time. However, friction will turn into conflict when the concept of guest and host is not being understood in the broader sense. A modern successful nation might resent that population overflow is being directed to its shores by primitive peoples who do not care to manage their immediate affairs of overcrowding but unload their problems somewhere else, do not conform to restrain their own activities if given assistance and begin to burden that new nation with their enormous onslaught of population production, sooner or later eroding any living standard as they had done prior, before leaving the shores of their land which was bursting in its seams with the creation of massive numbers of their kind, first depleting the food supplies and wasting away the last resources their homeland was capable of producing. The seed for never-ending conflict begins to grow into brutal confrontations: a scenario which is cleverly avoided by many religious doctrines.

The understanding of his very self, the knowledge of mind and body and the interaction of many other influences have to be considered in order to sustain human success as it presents itself so diversely on this globe, in our nations and least not last in our families. It is, therefore, that these thoughts pertaining to the strength we can generate from within us relate to a basic understanding of human affairs, that: **success and failure have a prescription which rests somewhere within the bosom of nature**.

It is only man's intellect alone which is capable of understanding, wrestling away that force of nature which has governed him for the past hundred million years, and which is still being challenged by the occurrences nature is so capable of redirecting against this, his effort to succeed, without causing harm to himself and others.

# Chapter IV

♦

# Negativity and the Subgram

"...none of us can ever be totally without positive influence for any length of time..."

**Ching T'suo**, sitting peacefully or meditating, is an exercise which affects the mind, calming it and training it at the very same time. The mere act of causing one to sit down (for whatever reason) in itself constitutes a collaborate effort on the part of the one who is difficult to reach.

Noise, in its very natural state, is in opposition to quiet and calm; therefore, it stands to reason that the mind is kept away from distracting sounds, especially if they are harsh and dominating ones. The human mind can deal easier with peace and quiet than cope with the harsh sounds which cross into the high decibels of the sound meter. Noise, in itself, even if enjoyed for a short while, rearranges certain natural concepts. As it can excite if coupled with rhythm, it has a quality which unearths the primitive, the basic behaviour in man. Primitive man without restricting himself by a code of conduct would end up in ecstasy and subsequent exhaustion. Though a certain type of noise can be beneficial to man, since it assists him in the pursuit of happiness, it becomes detrimental to

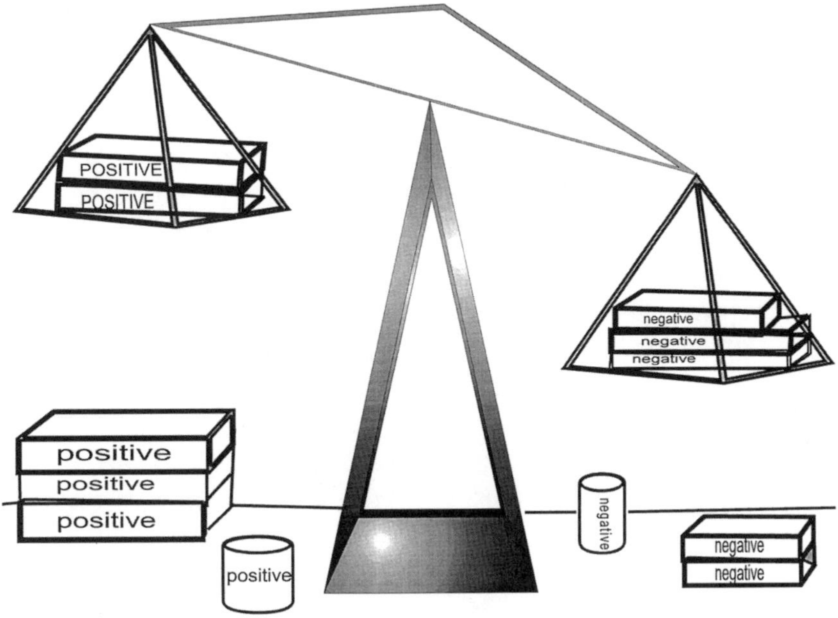
POSITIVE
POSITIVE
negative
negative
negative
positive
positive
positive
positive
negative
negative
negative

him if it does not balance his emotional needs. Somewhere into all of this enters the human mind. It is, therefore, that some persons will show a much higher tolerance toward the abuse of noise than others - or it might only appear to be so. Living organisms, however, are restricted by how, how many, how long and what interferences are brought to them.

A certain type of noise conditioning can be observed with many people. Finally, upon leaving the highly competitive city with its dense traffic, pollution, etc., many people set out to travel into the "recreational parks" of the nation; but here, bar a few exceptions, another phenomenon is being observed. The same people who actually set out to escape are taking their habitual surroundings with them: the noise, the rush, the drive to succeed by means of competing no longer in the workplace but very much so on the water while skiing, while driving to the place of rest and while sightseeing, leaving many hundred miles per day behind them fervently collecting the stickers of "famous places"! It is fair to assume, depending upon many other factors as yet, that many of these people will return exhausted from their holidays, using a more colloquial term "shot"; but, if asked will announce with great enthusiasm that they had a real good time and have never felt better. It is true that excitement can be in its very own way "rejuvenating" but mainly for persons who lack that excitement at their place of work: for instance, the librarian would wish to climb a mountain or race a speed boat; and if he has not done so already may be advised that he should. Since the public has been made aware of poor eating habits, it has become difficult to sell them butter or other products (eggs, etc.) in excess thought to potentially cause a higher accumulation of cholesterol in the blood. It is fair to say that the general public has become very health conscious and in many cases is so well-informed that some physicians have to do their homework to keep up with their patients who have proven to be well read when it comes to their personal well-being. Unfortunately, stress (and its devastating side-effects) is not understood by the general public as well as their daily diets are. If it could be achieved that larger groups of people would practice a certain type of "Mental Hygiene" together with new behavioural concepts, many of our citizens would live a happier and longer life and billions of dollars would remain in the profit margin before being wasted on the unnecessarily sick and grief stricken, in the end even eliminating the dreaded "manager's disease", keeping the entrepreneur alive, the one unique individual who creates new opportunities for many more citizens.

Stress, a symptom of the modern society, was never really understood as having a devastating impact upon the well-being of our species. Previous generations lived, in general, a much more contented life. Modern motivation tells us that we all have the "right stuff" to become rich or successful and, by some divine law in this universe, each and everyone believes that he could be that person. As a result, the general public strives for goals which remain largely unachievable because in order to succeed one has to understand certain natural laws. It does not matter whether one is highly motivated since motivation only creates a small bridge toward that goal which lies on the other side of the "River of Plenty". Since we allegedly all are capable of doing "great things" (whatever that means), we will have to understand the nature of

53

man: that he competes and will continue to do so in any society, may it be structured as it wishes. It is of course immediately apparent that if all can succeed, according to the new mental gymnasts, also all will be in opposition, making it a very difficult society to live in if such an achievement could be accomplished! At this point already is it clear that this is simply not so. A large group of our fellowmen wish to have less responsibility than the rest of us and rightly so. Each and every human being has his own make-up and history, a certain blueprint which influences his personality. This blueprint can differ vastly from the next. It is, therefore, no wonder that some persons do not require any motivation whatsoever and others are in dire need of it. Since it is here where a wide range of inconsistencies exist, modern industrialized man simply motivates all his employees whether they are in need of incitement or not. Motivation consumes energy, mind energy, and this energy has to come from somewhere. It is no small wonder that many persons simply run out of that force. Meeting them immediately after a promotional session has ended, all of the present persons are inspired and ready to attack their shortcomings, willing to climb any mountain. The exsurgent masses however differ from each other already by the next day.

The blueprint of our past is that which is generally referred to as being our so-called make-up. Many of these formed "units" of the blueprint are subliminal entities and as such are primarily responsible for the make-up of the personality of the individual. To hope to change these **subgrams**, these imprints, to form a new outlook, to simply adapt a new way, to follow a new "blueprint", is not all that easy to accomplish since the individual has to deal with his own make-up, his blueprint, to which he may not have access at all. He may follow an idea and wish to become successful but since **his make-up might not contain the steps with which to climb,** he will begin to climb on his own and fall short: he will fall back to that to which he was programmed by the many years of all that which made him prone to failure. The mind, aware as it might present itself to any person, undergoes a structural building process. Everything that is stored by the subconscious mind over the many thousands of days of instruction forms a blueprint of that past including any specific instructions or experiences. Adding the word *experience* only enlarges the sphere of all which has exerted influence on the mind over a certain period of time.

This imprint in the mind is accepted as being a **subgram**, a memory block, sketching past experiences from which the personality has been formed over the years. Since there are an overabundance of memories being stored in the mind of every person, we are only interested in the information which lends itself to the forming of good habits, ideas which are leading to self-elevation. Negative imprints are in opposition to the survival capability which we, for better understanding, will call here a service mechanism which has been equally placed into each and every human being from the time of birth by the Creator. **Nature equips every human being, for that matter every living creation on earth, with what is needed to survive and succeed on their own.**

Since disabling disorders are rare and not a common affliction of the majority of the human race, they become the exception; the rest of us, being of sound mind and will, are guided away from our path by the influences and occurrences we experience from the first day onward, from the day on which we are born. Good experiences enhance the capability to succeed (success does not breed failure); whereas failure appears to breed more failure only.

Some constitutions tell us that we are born equal, which in a legal sense is welcome; however, certain genetic information already exists within us. Being born of parents who had histories of depression (not referring to any known mental disorder) because, for instance, of being unemployed for the main part of their lives, will not really affect the newly born since the genes are not affected by such occurrences; however, the alcoholic and the drug user could change a healthy genetic composition. All new life is equipped to succeed no matter where it presents itself as long as the place is safe enough to begin to grow. However soon, following the first steps, the surrounding will start to make an impression upon the young mind. The state of the surroundings are instrumental in the instruction the newly born mind receives from such an environment to either flourish or to wilt away: in modern terms to succeed or to fail. There are, of course, exceptions to this rule but modern science has an overabundance of case histories to prove the effect that surrounding (and occurrences) can directly have on the well-being of the forming life. One should understand the seriousness of such observations and the findings, which, probatum est, command our attention if we wish to comprehend what transpires within the remotest regions of the mind of each and every human being.

There is the report where the eager parent forced the child to swim at a young age. The cold water left a mark in the mind of the child. This incident was recorded in the memory of the brain along with many others to come. The five senses begin to mentally record any and all information they can conceive and if the greatest impression is negative (in this case fear), the personality of a human being is slanted toward a less positive direction.

The cognoscente young adult may continue to falter and sway in his outlook and attitude if so influenced in the early part of his life. He would have to be motivated: motivation a method by which an outsider attempts to condition the mind of another person deemed to be functioning with a diminished desire for achievement.

The Neo Ch'an concept leans on the Buddhist tradition which holds that experience alone, direct living experience, is a true method of relating knowledge to its disciples. Outmoded as this concept might appear in the modern world, it has some fundamental value. On an interreligious basis it will provide an escape from the dilemma the past holds, locked deep inside and within the chambers of our minds. Since not all the information which directs our lives is of a subconscious nature, does it also become important to understand the cognizant part, the part we can remember and understand best as experience does so well. A bad experience, which can be remembered, will remain that until by means of reason it will be analyzed and accepted and neutralized in one's mind. Only then can good judgement occur if it is born of this consequence, providing the person desires to seek progress and wishes to overcome such a bad experience. It is in the interest of the survival mechanism, a service mechanism, to warn the mind, the conscious as well as the subconscious one, and to condition it to never forget an experience which made an impact upon it.

Depending on the emotional state and the make-up of the person involved, destiny begins to direct them onto a negative or positive path.

What we here are referring to as destiny, per se, is indeed nothing else than the forces of nature trying to balance themselves along the way. The Chinese talk of the Yin and Yang, the male and female or the weak and the strong, the power which seeks to level and balance the two opposites. A human being whose subgram holds negative information will not be able to do this on his own, simply by being too much out of balance with the rest. Different forms of help and assistance are needed.

Our emotions are the main guiding device within us, linked inseparably to the brain and the subgrams stored there, many of them. The teacher who tells the young boy that he better forget about becoming a scientist because his mathematics are hopeless will make a lasting impression on a sensitive child, so much so that in fact the child will choose to never enjoy his class again. It is important here to understand, firstly, that the teacher said this in front of the rest of the class and secondly the fashion in which he said it. Many such occurrences are being stored in "subliminal prints" or the word coined here for the first time as a subgram (sub stemming from subliminal or subconscious) and retained by all of us. Thus, the young man who decides to enter university to better himself will fail more readily if his make-up is mainly negative in nature.

In order to begin to change and help such persons, it is important that they learn to understand something of their own subgrams from their own personal history and then only from a new point of view altogether. Our subgram can place itself centripetal to our emotions and whatever it entails will influence the emotional force or the lack of it. Backing, support, trust and belief are all so closely related to the success mold of the mind that **none of us can ever be totally without positive influence for any length of time**, especially not if the subgram has been engraved adversely by previous occurrences, long before we had any knowledge or influence upon it. Our well-being stems mainly from our self-esteem: our own outlook (image) which we have consciously or subconsciously toward ourselves. We telegraph to others our intentions by the way in which we approach or cope with a subject matter, by the fashion in which we carry ourselves while walking across a room, by the way we look or the way we dress. Animals can detect, by their sense of smell, whether the opposite species has fear: the overproducing glands reveal that fear through their secretion. The world of man is that of a living specimen where most of the basic protective functions are still intact. One person appears sympathetic and another does not. Animal and man alike, however, can disguise their intentions and the survival mechanism can equip some species with formidable gifts. A "con" or confidence man will always be extremely nice, flexible and most of all believable; otherwise, he could not succeed. His survival instinct is motivated by the skill he conceives to own and which he has tested on others numerous times. Knowing that man's intentions are being communicated by his gestures so can they also be hidden by his intellect. Such is the case for all people since no one wishes to appear unsuccessful when questioned or tested. Even the negative person takes umbrage when so confronted.

For an everyday approach we should learn to identify three main types of human being who can be termed to possess negative, downbeat personalities:

**Type I**: the **Immobile Negative** - *cannot be readily changed*

**Type M**: the **Mobile Negative** - *difficult to change*

**Type S**: the **Searching Negative** - *changeable to succeed*

Since all three types can be reached and programmed to change their ways, a distinction is being made here as to the grade of effort it would take once communication has been established in order to achieve change. But remember: **any or all change can only be achieved with the cooperation of the individual**.

The above mentioned categories do not necessarily fit a strictly scientific evaluation nor do they have to. Simplification will align us with these more common categories while other types, here not mentioned, should seek out direct professional assistance since their individual make-up would be too complex to induce behavioral change which could provide lasting advantages.

**Type I** has a subgram which is entrenched deeply, probably by a distinct environmental cause. In many cases this type of being functions on a very fragile emotional frequency.

**Type M** is a being who is commonly satisfied with his lot.

However, in comparing himself to others who are successful, he becomes discontent yet displays aggressiveness toward change. He will seek out friends or family and talk of his misfortunes extracting mental energy from others for his benefit thus draining the mental energy of the positive being. Without the constant help of others, he will not truly succeed.

**Type S** is understood to be the most common type of negative person. He is the one who is the searching type, trying to explain to himself why failure keeps haunting him wherever he goes.

The categories, as they are shown here, have been created in order to uncomplicate the subject matter. Type I has many classifications which could be found between the first mentioned group and that of the M gradation as well as the Type M group has a definite connection to the Type S referred to as the searching type, while all are again interrelated to each other.

The latter type designated S is the type with which the North American society is riddled for it is believed that nine persons out of ten belong to this type. The act of searching, however, in itself is already a positive drive. This is the type of person who can be reached best by practicing mental hygiene in the context of Neo Ch'an mind training.

All three groups are believed to have been given a fairly normal childhood, lacking major deprivation. As soon as special events enter the life experiences of those individuals, all three categories would behave in accordance to such exposures; however, each on their own would maintain a certain proportional relationship to their above outlined, basic trends.

The Type I, with better than normal outside influence, would change his trend slightly for the better or, if a more detrimental influence was being exerted upon his life experience, a subsequent more serious negative subgram would hamper the attempt to change this individual. This observation would apply in proportion to the M and S group as well.

We may assign the "remote capability" to be positive to the Type I person, as we have learned to understand their general make-up as being of the opposite nature. While each and every human being will show signs of positivity, regardless of whether he could be classified as belonging to these mentioned groups, if observed on a wide spectrum, the negative person does something entirely different with a positive impulse and, of course, the positive person can naturally show some negative tendencies. *The decisive turning point will be found in observing how each of these opposites handles themselves when making decisions.* Their entire imagination is still dominated by their subgram, be it negative or positive in nature.

The psychologists may look somewhat differently at this notion but in the end all the scientific talk will have come to the same conclusion: that **positive minds differ from negative minds very remarkably**.

It may be quite comprehensible that the Type I indicates by speech and behaviour some interest in an uplifting experience. After all, no one really dislikes something which is enjoyable or beneficial, for example, an offer of a well paying job, etc. To receive a gift or to be congratulated upon an achievement falls within the realm of success and cannot be found in the working process toward accomplishment: they occur at the end of the line after the work has been done.  Such occasions are handled by most persons with joy, since no real effort is needed to indulge in them; subsequently, it is here where the negative type will appear positive to the rest of us.  However, if Type I persons would have to embark on their own free will and accord upon anything which requires personal effort in order to succeed, if they have to get involved in a certain demanding action, they will find many reasons as to why it would not be good for them to do so.  Their self-esteem is ill placed within them and will reveal a certain disorder when observed.  They are very positive in their reasoning but  much moreso in their defense, before friends and loved ones, as to why they in fact resent being hired, employed, engaged or as to why, in the end, no one would give them a chance anyway.

The Type I is known for heavy "leaning".  Some of these individuals can be highly intelligent even quite unassuming but when it comes close to the state of avoiding to get involved they are shockingly innovative.  They like good pay but fear the responsibility which goes along with better pay.  Their friendly but meek smile usually gives them away ahead of time.  Offer them a negative observation regarding the job for which they had just applied and they will quickly take the first opportunity to opt out! Their deep rooted disorder affects the co-workers who sense the weak make-up of such an individual, feeling the downdraft which such a pessimistic person emits by some strange but natural law. Many Type I persons will make it through university and get their degrees but primarily due to the total backing of others.  Within the same family the girl is very happy and willing to advance herself, while the brother comes home from the faculty and complains about his difficult studies telling, day after day after day, that he would fail because too many students are enrolled, most of them from wealthy families. But day in and day out, the sister reverses his opinion and in many instances not without extreme friction. Upon telling the brother how great he really is and that he, especially, would have nothing to fear (after all he had excellent marks in his tests), he finally receives his degree; only however, after having drained the sister of her last mental resources, she now struggling to barely succeed herself. Type I leaches off the mental energies of others and advances only with their backing. As long as the brother finds no other *backer*, he will stand still: his world has nothing to offer any longer until someone else feels sorry and restarts the entire momentum. If married, he will appear weak and if the other being is of a positive nature both characters will collide: the positive person, rejecting the outlook of the partner, gets tired of hearing why things will not work in opposition to why they could in fact work. In most cases, the Type I carries a strong imprint along making it difficult to foster happiness since their outlook toward the future will be extremely dim. Generally, these types specialize in the judging of others in order to find mistakes, thus re-enforcing their own shortcomings.

The Type M person differs only in the degree of severity of these discussed symptoms. The M type, however, can be reached and in time changed to adapt a different attitude. His subgram is not as deeply rooted as that of Type I.

This now brings us to Type S, an individual who constitutes the largest portion of the general population. The latter person is the easiest to motivate and will, with some understanding and work, suddenly make it on his own, providing of course that he has the skill, basic intellect and rationale as ready equipment available on his road to conquest. If these are lacking, he will still not succeed but become a burden to the working place for, being ill-equipped and thus incapable of forging on, he will in the end still fail.

These categorized types function all according to their additional inherited characteristics, be they good ones or be they of another nature. Their future path through life will be directed by the blueprint of their make-up, the subgram. The subgram stores inside as well as outside conditions, that is to say experiences, into the memory bank of the brain. Inside conditions are conditions with which we are already bestowed at birth and outside conditions are all those which are added to these characteristics, forming a subgram. In the end, the inside as well as the outside factors will appear in the subgram, constituting a total unit within our emotional structure, forming a character which is being directed from the innermost regions within us. If this is true, **it should be in fact possible to change anyone's negative characteristics into the opposite ones**, providing that one has the knowledge, the key in order to do just that.

# Chapter V

◆

# The Most Unusual Secret within the Universe of our Mind

"... the mind has the key to the body and
it holds, therefore, the road to its access
within itself."

Many of the success oriented business promoters are not really involved with their public after a motivating session has come to an end. In almost all cases the thrust of the talk is centered upon demonstrating how someone can get rich by adhering to their program, which naturally has a price. Literally millions of people have bought such books and tapes and begun to experiment on their own only to find out in the long run that they, ninety-nine point nine percent of them, remain still as poor as before. The only ones who in fact are doing well are the operators who sold the books and tapes in the first place. There are several factors which must be seriously considered before embarking upon any such program in order to have the proper outlook and understanding of this subject matter.

A certain requirement of honesty with oneself is mandatory. One has to be rational about one's capabilities otherwise the most seriously imagined desire or plan will not come true. A person wishing to be like a bird, wanting to fly, will only succeed if he can substitute all that which makes flight possible, that he understands the theory of flight, observes flight and constructs aids to obtain flight; for, believing alone will not cause any person to get airborne! Natural law has it that if one jumps from a roof, one never goes up but rather down, down, down! So **rationality in proportion to the tasks to be achieved has to prevail**.

The second, but most important, concept to follow is **not to forfeit one's character in order to achieve anything**: the conscience of a human being has to remain fully intact and should not become self-serving. It is here where Neo Ch'an mind training differs from all. One self-styled psychologist became wealthy by telling the criminals that society has caused their affliction: he was able to create a scheme by which the individual conscience was being erased and therefore it was possible for the first time to blame others, society, for their misfortunes. This is a rather profitable but dangerous practice to free such individuals from their conscience, the only faculty and connecting link to integration, remorse within the depth of the soul of a human being, by which most who have done wrong can be brought back into a civilized society. **Pure theory of law cannot be written without that the conscience is being considered as a primary catalyst for the re-entering into society.**

# The Human Mind - an ingenious marvel of creation

The mechanics, by which the mind functions, are best found in the nervous system. In the typifying of certain human beings, as done here, forming distinct classes for quick reference, it must be understood that these three types are deemed to be of a normal state of mind, and as such, subject to their own specific subgram. If any of these cited types suffer from mental disorders it would be fair to say that any motivation, other than that which would come by way of a trained scientist, would fail to alter their subgram, if it in fact can be changed at all. The nervous system relies upon certain cells which are responsible for transmission of information through a vast array of functions, either bodily ones or mental ones. Somewhere, amidst all of these functions, a general balance between all stimuli involved must take place in order to sustain health. Nerve cells conduct the passing on of information in one direction only from the apex of the dendrites (a process of neurons which carry nerve impulses to the cell) and then from the cell body along the axon (efferent process of a nerve cell) which somewhere terminates in a dendrite cluster of more cells. Nerve cells are structured in a three-fold manner: first and foremost, the brain is an arrangement of more than ten billion such nerve cells, which are interconnected with each other, passing from here on to the spinal cord, the second most noticeable arrangement of such cells and then, finally, the third group which is referred to as the peripheral system, where nerves branch in many lines reaching through the human body.

From the Greek physician Galen to Sherrington as well as from the works of the ancient Chinese doctors much knowledge has been gathered about the human mind. It was learned that the mind and the subsequent physical and mental functions are extremely intricate but totally interrelated. A "reflex" displays the simplest electrical circuit in our body. There are certain main nerve cells which perform specific functions as the sensory cell does, passing its information (frequency) on to the motor cell. As much as the complexities are being understood, a measureless amount of unknowns remain yet to be discovered. Many of the prime circuits in the brain have proven to be difficult to trace. There is a possibility that many millions of circuits exist, each dependent upon the other, some being capable of substituting in part if others fail. Much is known as to how the impulses from the brain travel and by what kind of chemical arrangement they report back to the brain cells. The ear, the eye and all the other sensatory devices report continuously to these cells and interact by innumerable interconnections with impulses which vacillate several thousand times over within the flash of a second. Imagine, for example, it is possible for the olfactory nerve cells to detect mercaptan, a sulphur compound, by dividing a *fiftieth* billion parts of air: a work which no modern high tech instrument is as yet capable of. As much as science has unearthed from the pit of the unknown, much more is there to be evaluated and learned and it is astonishing how little as yet can be used and applied to assist man in his struggle to become free of certain devastating diseases. One fact is true: **if the mind is in disarray it stands to reason that much of the body will have a difficult time to remain functional in order to assure a good**

**life**.

      We have learned to understand that two major spheres of awareness exist: the conscious and the subconscious and perhaps even others which still remain hidden from our present methods of scientific measurement. Since Freud, Adler and Jung have wrestled to categorize the effects the mind produces, and since they have made a major breakthrough along this difficult pathway, entire books have been compiled just to understand the new language which is being applied to all that which has been explored and discovered. There is the unconscious mental action pinned against the conscious one: the voluntary facing the involuntary motor action; and least but not last the circuits which function deep in the unknown, the motoring devices which are not reachable by the conscious mind, responsible to our visceral organs. Even in anger or distress one cannot address the heart in such a way as to stop it from beating so rapidly. **However, in an indirect way, through stress and psychosomatic stimuli, this can change, since breathing alone set apart from any other living function of ours, has both conscious as well as subconscious qualities within its functions, as if a bridge from the conscious to the subconscious actually exists.** Aside from this, the mind has no direct access though it has sufficient admission in order to secure a well functioning heart. Yet another group of nerve cells, motoric in nature, carries on such activities as supervising the heart and other organs, regulating blood pressure and body temperature; and even the digestion, referred to as the autonomic system, functions along the sympathetic and parasympathetic nerve strands which reach from the back deep into the human body. The work these nerves

70

perform is absolutely astounding as they are responsible for the viscera, glands and even cause the arteries and blood vessels to expand and contract. Interchanges from the subconscious to the conscious occur when the nerve cells report to the conscious level: a disorder may present itself in the form of pain or nausea and, depending upon the nature of the underlying cause, much can be at stake.

The mind functioning by itself marvels the wonders in the universe and yet is, on the other hand, very much dependent upon the rest of the structural physical body. If its interchanges are not kept in balance even the best trained mind will begin to falter, become ineffective and finally fade away like a drifting cloud, never to be seen again. **The mind, alike the body, adheres to certain functioning laws of nature. An interaction between both becomes, in time, mandatory for the sustenance of lasting health**. New medical research has learned that inactivity, that is physical inactivity, causes a chemical deprivation in the brain; thus, in most human beings inducing depression. Many disorders of the mind have such a basic origin and are, therefore, not serious in nature. However others, depending upon their source, can be serious and destructive: some can become incurable altogether. Since we cannot address all human mind functions at the very same time and since we can neither cure all physical disorders at the very same moment, it stands to reason to learn about the most pressing involvements which can affect our well-being. One thing we believe to be true is that: **the mind has the key to the body and it holds, therefore, the road to its access within itself**.

The person who avoids exercise while knowing that he

should exercise does not seem to be reaching his very own mind; or, if he is being distracted by pertinent worries (cost, time, etc.) he does not seem to understand the relationship between cost and well-being. To be healthy and remain so should be worth some investment. The scientist of the medical branch of psychology, psychiatry, can probe into the mind of a patient, but only if the patient wishes him to do so. Though most persons believe they know themselves very well, it has been established, however, that this is really not so. Our present day scientists have answers for most of our disorders while at the very same time they have none at all for some diseases. The dreaded visit to see a psychiatrist stems from the medieval days where witchcraft and superstition haunted the mentally ill. All diseases have an origin as do disorders and faults. Firstly, they are somewhere tied into the cosmos of the mind before they appear anywhere else. The key to the state of health of the entire human being, barring a few exceptions, can be found here. It is therefore mandatory that:

*if we wish to address our minds, we must pay homage to the entire human body and not only address one part, thus remaining one-sided, out of balance with the rest.*

| Impressions | These are powerful images which create impulses and affect the nervous system and the mind in one way or another and, yes, there is a good and a bad way. What appears |

to be good for one institution or person may not be good for the rest of the nation. Advertising, for instance, is the most powerful mind shaper of modern day man. Here, armies of scientists are massed together in order to secure results: the world of high finance somewhere centers around results. Based upon the first observation, this is easy to comprehend. However, in the struggle to do good for the rest the result comes out very differently. The mass of the population is totally unaware as to how they are being manipulated; in fact, they do not believe that it is at all possible to be manipulated; but the next few lines will prove them wrong.

Modern advertising has within it the capability to be the most ruthless method ever used to induce man to spend his money. Here, as well, is an underlying cause of stress to be found. It is not necessarily poverty which causes stress but rather how to pay for the new car when the "due date" comes near. The person had been, over time, conditioned to his state of poverty and was comfortable with his *poorness* but could not adjust to the responsibility attached to the inability to pay. Since media advertising began under its own code of ethics and as advertising expanded its scientific understanding of man, was it mainly with the assistance of psychology that certain events began to overtake an entire industry. At the symbolic level, laws cannot be applied any longer. Yet through thought association, a concept that is well understood in the world of psychology, one can sell the most hideous drives or

73

dreams which control the subconscious of each and every human being. One does not have to have a "dirty mind" at all if one is being directed by the media to that which makes us function, and of course especially so if one is unprepared: treating the human being like an animal, nude scenes are concealed in ice cubes and even acts of bestiality occurring at the symbolic level remain hidden, ready to be used at will against us. Children's dolls are sold at Christmas time, four letter words hidden in the facial folds. Since the mind works in wondrous ways the letters can even be placed upside down: the mind will correct what is being presented to it. Remember, if someone reaches you a newspaper the wrong way with the letters facing upward, you will turn the paper around. The mind after all turns the paper around: the signal to the arm which follows that wish is coming from the brain in the first place. The subconscious mind will read letters or identify symbols if they are presented for such purpose.

Sociology, psychology are not really cherished since they mainly appear within the confines of lecture halls. Generally, they supply an administrative purpose for governments. **Unfortunately, psychology, the science which was to save man, has begun to exploit him.** Media exploitation is based upon the politically structured financial support system. Media exploitation occurs in the world of print as well as in the world of moving images, mainly television and at times even in the entertainment sector, movies. Of course, the North American population is not the only one under attack. In other countries, the media is used equally as efficiently for better emotional and political control. Several works by conscientious scientists have been written but have never really

74

penetrated the marketplace or reached the households. The masses are occupied with one thing only...where their benefit can be obtained: this the scientists know as well. As an enormous pressure by the business world is exerted on whether goods can be sold quickly with the best or highest possible profits, the rest of society has to follow since the entire system of goods and services is tied to money, the oldest concept of well-being. The methods of subliminal advertising are difficult to monitor. Prior to using these methods, the industry has already done its footwork, seeking out legal advice for its benefit while the citizen is still unaware of the conspiracy. As laws were unable to stop crime, they have in turn however caused crime to become more adaptable. Laws can now be circumvented, depending upon the intellect, connections and other means man has in store for such a purpose. Fortunately, it is difficult to corrupt and control an entire people in a democratic setting for any length of time particularly if they are either aware of the techniques being used or if their moral will is of such nature that it can resist a certain corruptive influence. In order to do that, however, first the mind must be made aware of the attempt. **It is in fact as if a universal law within us can protect us from abuse provided we put it into action**.

Our modern world exerts a massive amount of influence upon our modern minds. It is not only that we are manipulated by the media for the benefit of their sales, there is political influence applied as well and there are all the other countless occurrences which constitute a daily cycle from noise to all the fears which we must deal with in order to keep on living without much harm befalling us.

Most abnormal behaviour is generally classified as either psychotic or neurotic behaviour: the neurotic behaviour comes closest to the normal state of mind. The neurotic person has still a good contact with reality whereas the psychotic one has lost all relationship to reality. If compared in numbers, most of our citizens are mildly neurotic without much harm coming to them and society in general. Only if the neurotic state remains unchanged for a longer time period can the matter become a serious affair. Neurotic causes, as widely accepted, are mainly environmental in nature. They are caused by stress and strain of which life seems to supply an abundance. A typical neurotic is a person who carries noise (radio) along, listening to it without really knowing what is being said or played; yet, he will have a difficult time turning it off. As soon as the quietness sets in, he will become uneasy and feel lost. For him noise is a *backer*, a support. If more burdening effects are not added to this, he will be fine though not necessarily his neighbors to whom he may cause a great deal of stress! Some neurotics are known to be perpetually late, hopelessly forgetful or exhibit a tidiness which would drive a normal person "up the wall". Some will manipulate others cleverly to achieve praise or block unpleasant occurrences from their own mind. Some behave in this manner because they are generally timid or believe they are undeserving or seek to cover unpleasant things by means of redirecting their emotions until they, somewhere along the road, may lose control over what they are doing, depending upon the seriousness of that neurosis. In most such cases they can be cured by simply seeking out a specialist, a scientist who learns to understand the cause of such neurotic behaviour while talking to the subject.

The bulk of the population, the ones who are only mildly affected in such ways, can learn to apply the methods of Neo Ch'an mind training as long as they are honest to themselves and remain rational about that which they want to achieve through it. A person being mentally ill already cannot be helped by anything which is being directed on a voluntary basis. Only medical, professionally trained help can redirect or minimize all that which is needed to benefit the patient. Unchecked neurotic conditions can cause mental disorders. One condition in particular would be schizophrenia which is often not even recognizable in many persons as they function alongside the rest of us. They are usually listless, dull and indifferent to outsiders. Armies of them drift amidst society in every country of the world. From catatonia to paranoia and from hebephrenia to mania (or manic depression), many of these diseases depend upon the emotional state of the mind or relate to genetic defects or other causes which are brought into play. Of course, least but not last we have the psychopath. Here, we have a person who outwardly appears highly intelligent but seems to lack emotional depth, having no real concern as to whether he is doing right or wrong and even less concern for the consequences of his actions. Since the study of the principles of Neo Ch'an Mind Training deals mainly with the onslaught of daily occurrences, mind boggling challenges, it does not lend itself to heal mentally ill persons or cope with serious character disorders. It, however, can assist the fairly normal person to gain access to his own mental faculties and free himself of the many shortcomings and mind directing influences which affect us all.

**77**

Most tasks we take on in life depend upon our capabilities from within. Some persons will not even begin to perform a very basic task as they hold the firm belief inside themselves that they are just "not cut out" for this particular act. Their self-confidence, actually the lack of it, will redirect them elsewhere. It is here where the first stone has to be turned if we wish to learn how to become truly, lastingly successful, either in dealing with stress or anything else which influences the mind adversely. **The first step in order to achieve this is to establish a personality which is more capable of dealing with impressions, information or other messages which are reaching the mind.** The concept of Neo Ch'an Mind Training is a composition of the physical and the mental aspects in this universe, directing our attention to the fact that two major attributes are hidden within this concept. Any attempt to train the mind only while neglecting the body is equally as one-sided as training the body only without thinking of the one, the directing force, to which most of our actions are connected - the mind.

Beginning here, addressing the mind, our emotions, we will learn about the most simple secrets in the entire universe: we will arrive at a new crossroad and find the incentive to do all the things we never thought of or change the outlook, the conception we had of ourselves. The first door which we will have to open then is that of being **willing to listen and learn**, to pry away some deep honesty from our souls and accept the idea of becoming a new person, if so needed, to follow all that which shall be explained here to you. Our attention shall be directed mainly toward ourselves, the way we think; because it is here where the first stepping stone to success, lasting health and happiness, is to be found. Self-esteem, a word seldom ever analyzed, was left as something other persons possessed who could afford to exhibit and utilize it, because they also were able to back their actions with their wealth. Thus arrived the myth that anyone else had to simply take their natural place and wait for miracles to happen. If there is in fact one miracle, it resides within the knowledge of how to achieve a healthy level of self-esteem. The crossroads within our minds present themselves here: **thought should become rational action**. If there could be a map printed by which one would arrive at success, on which such a roadway would exist, we would still have to obtain the tools, the ways and the means, to find such a road and mark it in order to see where it leads.

**Since all the tools are within ourselves, since our mind supplies all the answers, it holds the key to our future.**

# Chapter VI

♦

# As People Think,
# So They Are

*"...our subgram will direct us to that
which was established before, no matter
whether good or bad..."*

At first sight this chapter title seems to be harsh in its
message. There is the person who can never get enough of
anything, the greedy type who even brags that he cannot help
himself - it is simply the way he functions. As greed may allow us
to obtain certain things, it is not a quality which necessarily permits
us to keep the things which we acquire by means of greedy actions.
Sir Isaac Newton might have phrased his famous dictum in another
direction. Here also, removed from the cosmos, it could well apply
because it is true, even in the interactions amongst living beings,
that *for each and every action there will be an equal and opposite
reaction.* Modern day motivation having its roots mainly in the
promotion of unreasonable desires, greed, can foster such "opposite
reactions". The act of being greedy carries with it a certain brand
of desire. If we examine the word desire in itself, its meaning can
be accelerated from basic or simple desires to bad and evil desires.

Greed is never good in nature: it denotes rather evil desires.

In order to begin on a well structured path toward success, we must have a definite mental impression of what we wish it to be: the thought must follow an *ethical* approach of conscience, because any and all achievements can only occur with the help of your fellowman. **There is no business, no true advancement, no religious thought or idea which can be used, arranged and passed on without that another living human being will appear somewhere along the way. It is the other person, people, in part, who make us succeed.** As they like us or dislike us, will we have to take our place in either succeeding or failing on our way toward our goal. Only here, in the understanding of this concept, lies the truth to success before anything else should be examined and discussed. We are taught that we must have a goal. It is not only the goal in itself and it never will be only this goal in itself which is important in our outlook; but rather how reasonably and how well we understand ourselves in progressing toward such a goal, a target which we have envisioned in our minds. Not only is the planning important but the total personal assessment of our self. The rainbow arch toward reaching and climbing the money tree might exist but mainly for the ones who are already established and are subsequently in possession of wealth. Some of these individuals can break certain rules more readily than others but beware, for the tree that grew the money at one time or other could easily begin to wilt away. As people are money oriented, they differ in their outlook toward it. If they have a good and healthy outlook, they might resent certain persons or operators who do not match their very own moral subgram. **Money alone does nothing permanent to anyone**

**for any length of time**. The free marketplace can be a very harsh turf for the ones who try to enter it the wrong way. A certain type of motivator will offer shortcuts to success, his entire book scribbled full with graphics and statistics as to how one can become rich by believing in wealth. The truth is, there are really no quick approaches to wealth or happiness other than by winning a lottery or receiving an inheritance; and even worse, yet, is it if things begin to fail that one continues to surge forward on the expense of others. The proverbial uplifting phrase, "Let's make some money", is an erroneous one, since it is a criminal offense to do so. As I said before, only the government may make money by printing it and thus anyone not working there has to earn it. (The governments dislike citizens who print money on their own!) To *earn* money and to live by the rules and succeed lastingly is a different task altogether. Remember: the news are filled with those who made their own rules along the way and ended their careers in the many overcrowded jails of the nation. Since we have already established that success is tied to a constant clear outlook, maintaining a good conscience in regards to that which we are doing, is it important to work with the cooperation of others. We can observe that most successful people live a spartanic life: they are, in general, very well organized, some actually outright disciplinarian in nature. As that may or may not be, we must begin with ourselves. Having a certain type of self-esteem, feeling good about oneself, being serious and still showing a smile is a difficult enough task for most persons to achieve. There is an entire subliminal structure within us which is directed by the simplest law in the universe. It is directed by two things: *How we feel and what we think of*

82

*ourselves*. These two discoveries seem to be so closely related to each other that they appear to be the same at first glance. They are not. If we do not feel good about ourselves we must delve into our past as to why we feel depressed whenever we contemplate our very own self. Our subgram, in fact, must also not think highly of ourselves either and that message travels outward, away from us to others who will perceive the results of our lack of belief, thought, idea, or whatever. If Albert Einstein was known to arrive barefoot in shoes for his lectures, because he simply forgot to address such a petty topic, it is another matter altogether. He could afford such "errors" being established on the scale of success, and his errors were obviously easily forgiven by others. On the other hand, it can be said with great certainty that if we would repeat such performance while talking to the president of a company from whom we seek employment, that person might as yet not be as forgiving. He will detect a lack of something which belongs to the very basic make-up of a civilized man. **Self-esteem is a state which projects our composure, our outlook, our worth to others**. To arrive barefoot in sandals for an important employment interview might simply relate our state of affairs to others. However, the account which we transmit of our capabilities will shrivel away by this very action, as if we were purposely tossing away the key to success!

## From Self-image to Self-esteem

Looking at ourselves then, **we have to address bad habit patterns and change them to become good habit patterns**. Having lived for many years with bad habit patterns this attempt will not be as easy as it might appear. We are branded with a subgram of exactly such information in our subconscious mind. The mind has dealt in a certain way with a specific habit for many years and a mere wish will not erase the subgram from the subconscious. *How then do we change the unchangeable?* It is important to understand that one's personal self-image marks out the road toward proficiency: what you deem you can achieve or do and what you think you cannot. On the other side then, if this is true, we can say also that if we change or alter this image we should be able to alter such preceding, negative subgram. Altering something means of course also to change something; but to alter is to change certain things in a certain way. **Altering leaves the original subject intact**. If a shoe is being altered, the sole or heal redone, the shoe is still recognizable: if the shoe is being changed it might still be there but much more difficult to perceive. Admittedly so, the difference does not really surface if one does not think about it. To change oneself is much more difficult than to begin to *alter* certain things we are speaking of. If a block is too big to handle, one should begin to chip away at it: sooner or later it will become something we can deal with and not remain an obstacle, an obstacle we thought we were unable to handle.

**In order to understand success one ought to know of**

84

**success.** Having seen nothing but failure from childhood on and having experienced the pitfalls and setbacks of the past, one remains ill-equipped to succeed. Such impressions will impede our determination to overcome the subgram which, as we have learned, is a part of us whether we like it or not. If, in fact, an unpleasant history was present in any person's life, one should be realistic about it and accept it as good reason why "things" were going wrong. **In order to bring change about one begins with the altering of one's ways.** For instance, in order to become a good commercial pilot one must have a basic understanding of mathematics so the knowledge that this was one's shakiest and worst subject back in school will surely not help. Positive thinking alone does not work if it is inconsistent with one's vision of oneself: the knowledge of a certain phobia, here the dislike of mathematics, has become attached to an occurrence long since past. The attempt to think positive alone will not erase that which has been with us for a very long time. **Past events, then, are somewhere, no matter how deeply hidden, a part of our make-up.** The ingredients of the past experiences determine our way of thinking, in part, our behaviour. We learn to speak of our image, the fashion in which we are being perceived by others. **The projection of our own self-image is sent from us across to the other human being**. If something is wrong within us, it stands to reason that we will project that as well to others. The self-image, in other words, must be coupled with a hopeful, positive outlook toward a certain situation if the right message is to be delivered to the next person. The negative person will be unable to free himself on his own from gloomy experiences and if he cannot override the established subgram which he carries around within himself, he will continue to send his faulty message to others, remaining stationary in his attempt to succeed. He has to alter all the negative influences with which his subconscious mind is afflicted. Before this can be achieved, another simple natural law should be understood.

The brain, in all its complexity, is designed to back any thought which is put there by us in a very precise way: a command which could cause harm is screened and prevented from becoming active, instead preferring to encourage all orders which have no apparent adverse impact on us. However, the mind becomes confused if hesitation, especially fearful hesitation, enters into its programming process. If so approached, it will begin to tip the scale and choose a more secure path directing us to that which has already been established or to the next, safest action known within ourselves. If such action stemmed from past experiences, even though they actually were bad ones, we will resort to seeking them out, as **our subgram will direct us to that which was established before, to that which was familiar, comfortable, no matter whether good or bad**.

A particular environment requires a certain adaptability on the part of any living being. It is here that the designer laid the seed for all the children of his flock to succeed. God equipped all, man and beast alike, to survive best in their immediate surroundings firstly. The survival mechanism, therefore, is present in each and every living being but it can be impeded by us long before it can do its work, particularly if we already think less of ourselves as we begin to mark our intentions, either to fail or to succeed. **The brain, alike the earth, does not care what is being planted in its**

**depth: it will return that which was planted** and if hope or positivism is being sown, the human mind, the brain will in time strictly adhere to this natural phenomenon, producing happiness and success.  If failure, fear, hesitation is offered, the harvest will equal that which was being planted: it will produce doom, destruction and disbelief and one's effort will end in ruin.

The psychologists have unfolded new books and more lessons and much more parables for us in order to understand all that which is so complex within us.  Having set out to aid man in his struggle with himself and in their search for the functioning of the unknown mechanics within us, many have failed to show a social conscience.  Working for the seller and producer (the consumer certainly does not pay them), they achieved an advantage over us, the consumer, having little knowledge as to the scope of the manipulative powers the media can assert.  Subsequently, they are burdening the medical profession with the fallout of their practices.  The industrial world knows by now how man functions, how he conceives himself best, identifying different types of peoples and changing their advertising messages, which are highly scientific in design, to produce results at almost any cost, to reach these types, good or bad, for their gain.

Dividing the conscious from the subconscious, they are benefitting from the scientific applications more than the citizen does.  Observed on a larger scale, it is true that most of the profits which are being extracted by these means are being returned to the consumer by raising his standard of living; unfortunately, at an enormous cost to the ethical and moral well-being of the general public.  The human idea, the dream and the struggle has no home in such a place where the scientists prepare the masses to devour the goods, present in an abundance of unimaginable quantities, while feeling and fulfilment have become tools of manipulation.  If man is not an apparatus and if he cannot be compared to one, he most certainly uses the mechanics, addressing his natural drives which are present within him,  to extract profit.  Since profit is the motoring drive in any healthy economy, good advertising should seek the cooperation of the consumer rather than resorting to manipulation.  Unfortunately, it most often resorts to using psychological trickery to subvert his conscious mind.  It is, however, interesting to note that: **it is difficult to direct human intention if the person who is being manipulated has knowledge of the method by which this is being done**.

In practicing Neo Ch'an Mind Training one learns to deal with the personal subgram, that part of the structural memory bank which stores all information mainly as experiences.  If we, for example, have not experienced true happiness, the brain will not know of it.  It is now much easier to understand why a certain upbringing can either assist a child or totally deprive it from succeeding: in fact, nothing else can be said, for it will fail before it succeeds.

| The Big Task | Any person wishing to embark on the road toward true success has to equip himself with a specific type of knowledge. |

Since the mind directs all, it stands to reason that one ought to begin here. About fifteen hundred years ago the legendary monk Boddhidharma made his own observations in this regard: whether to first train the mind or, on second thought, to begin with the training of the human body? Upon his arrival from India in the Middle Kingdom, he discovered that the Chinese monks were inadequate in both aspects of training. They were found to be unfit for meditational practice. Meditation, that is religious meditation, was very physically demanding, sitting sessions could last many hours: many of the monks fell ill whenever Boddhidharma insisted on a more rigorous participation by them. He, therefore, proceeded to introduce certain calisthenics which lent themselves for the preparation of mind training. The readiness of the body was to become a prerequisite for all future meditational practices from this time on until the decline of the monasteries occurred.

As the modern pragmatic world seeks quick results (which presents itself in a type of "quick fix" attitude), it has bypassed a fundamental truth which revealed that **body and mind are interrelated.** If the body is being put through its paces, it will follow the impulses of the orders stemming from the brain as long as the brain is being properly supplied by nutrients, sufficiently so as to sustain a certain, continuous demand - **the key ingredient for stable mental functioning is however mainly supplied through exercise only**, creating a valuable chemical in the brain which as yet

**89**

cannot be found in any nutrient available. Man, after all, is not a machine, he is an *emotional* animal; and, as such, fragile if he does not learn how to conduct his affairs to suit his needs. Since each and every industry has its own specific demands, it will therefore also have its very own problems. The worst problem, however, occurs when the individual arrives already at the work place under emotional strain. All the well meant innovations of the employer will be a waste of effort and resources. As much as a nice surrounding would mean to a well balanced person, able to enjoy the spacious hall and the new dining facility, a person being burdened by private problems will hardly notice that on which others will take delight.

The practice of Neo Ch'an Mind Training cannot eradicate certain social injustices but can deal with them on a specific and personal basis by addressing the individual directly, preferably before any personal disorder befalls him.

How to address the Subgram.. Physical exercise holds the key to our general well-being as bodily motion is linked to the essential chemical exchanges in a very direct way: changes which are of vital necessity in order to achieve long lasting health. Aside from the exercise which conditions most of our muscles, the heart, one of the most critical of the group, attains a most beneficial reward as good circulation provides a more efficient delivery process for the essential nutrients. Since the blood is the main transporting system for these crucial victuals, it also removes most of the poisonous by-products from our system. It appears that the body can do this best if the circulatory system is in an active state, especially then supplying the brain with the much needed oxygen. Physical activity, therefore, compliments our mind in its search for achievement. It is important to think of achievement in a very specific way. **True achievements lie in the many little things and deeds which surround us daily**. To be able to get out of bed while the urge to rest, to remain where it is warm and cozy, where shelter is foremost present, is in itself already a task for most persons. To change a habit, be it smoking or the chewing of fingernails, *early on* is a simple problem; it, however, becomes very serious and very real whenever the affliction persists. The alcoholic who begins to set himself a goal not to drink for the next year would have been better advised to rather set a goal for one day only, then add a day by day effort to this list until he achieves a week, a month and finally a year. Together with this goal must of course be the admission of personal fault in order to foster such an effort. Physical well-being is firstly connected to exercise and a wide range of sports should provide a pleasant enough setting in order to not deter that which was difficult to do in the first place. Man does not enjoy working alone. Whether he admits this or not, he or she will like to be surrounded with agreeable people, persons who share into a certain discipline. A ski hill does not differ from an indoor pool nor does a canoe ride differ from an outdoor

91

camping trip: whatever a person wishes to do, he should also be willing to enjoy it. Fanatic sports which provide stress should be avoided by persons who already are working in a stressful environment. An assembly line worker should refrain from boat racing and rather choose a canoe, seek quiet and measure the type of excitement he enjoys with more care. To worry about the place of work while being on a vacation is as silly as it is to pack a portable telephone for communication if one has previously worked as a telephone operator. To worry about anything at all over which one has no input is equally as silly and futile in the end. If worries befall us does it become important to learn to **do something about the cause of our worrying**. If this can be done, one has achieved something concrete. Anything else will fall short of a solution.

Let us return again, however, to our first priority, physical exercise. As soon as we have decided what to do, where to participate (governments spend millions of dollars in order to encourage us to participate in anything at all) we should also begin to learn to take time out. Especially if week after week demands a seemingly endless involvement of our mental faculties, it might be wise to equip ourselves more lastingly in order to cope with such abuse. To have pressure at work and to also be confronted with problems at home can prove to be devastating to our mind, especially if it is already burdened with a negative subgram. Even very well suited partners in marriage can find themselves in strife and discontent if stress, fear, worries, anxieties rob them of all their normal defenses, the courtesies with which God equips all loving souls. The patient wife will turn into a nag and the loving husband can become something he never dreamt of. New and strange rules appear: the otherwise compassionate wife might save money to such an unreasonable degree that she disallows her husband to join a tennis club because the membership fee is allegedly too high, never once considering the benefit to him or his health. Each and every golf club membership might appear to be costly at first glance but what of health and happiness? Since we never ever had to spend money for all the things which were given free to us at birth we do not really appreciate them either. The brain comes free, remember: it does not care what one teaches it, it will return that which was placed into it and if nothing is brought to it, the brain will do as little as possible and will remain content with all that to which it is being introduced until it becomes saturated with a certain type of message. The natural defensive part within us will suddenly take over and the best relationship can begin to falter. The once charming woman begins to care less for the man she married so happily a few years before. One partner will prefer to leave the house more often working harder out of sheer fear of being around the other nagging party. They will soon have little to say to each other, which as a matter of fact is one of the most devastating types of behaviour for any marriage. Instead of enjoying life, the other party will elect to sit at home, hawking the television set while consuming dinners in full view of the screen. The home box will become their conversation center, their friend and their mentor, and all that which makes life interesting, such as places, skating in a park or taking the children out for a pleasant walk will be forfeited. Soon they will no longer differentiate between good and bad programs and will lull themselves into oblivion following man's instinct, his curiosity as to what will come next or what the opposite channel might have to offer. With fifty or more channels to view, the evening will be full and the year become as short as a day and subsequently nothing will be achieved. If no achievement is being found, little fulfilment will follow. It is here where so many errors were made by the so-called "Rich and Famous" ones, most of them motivated by sheer greed, the ones who literally fell, so to speak, into money. These individuals are still drinking themselves to death and many of them are stalked by isolation and all that which promised success has turned into utter despair. In other words, **the affluent societies produce more suicides than the groups who live in abject poverty**. An astounding fact about which the success promoters seem to know so little.

The first step, thus, should be a small one in order to find one's own relationship to oneself, so very important if such an enterprise is going to actually change things for the better. Therefore, the first step to start one's conceptional ideal toward lasting success shall begin with the preparation and harmonizing of body and mind through Purposeful Meditation - a method of mind training involving the basic understanding of the importance of self-esteem through balancing the mind and body. It will only then be equipped to embark on a lasting adventure, an adventure which will secure any success once planned upon this base.

# Chapter VII

♦

# The Path to Inner Strength

The Ch'i is a force of vital life energy and can be directed by the mind but not contained by it. Since many persons are ascribing to it a supernatural phenomenon, it is just the same a very real force which can be sensed and directed by the mind. This force travels through us and leaves us without doing anything if it is not directed: it behaves like the waves of light spreading everywhere. Without being capable of focusing it, it will have no strength within us; however, if channelled it will move immovable objects and overcome hurdles and obstacles never before imagined. It is in all likelihood the same source of energy of which the Pharoahs knew. After all, the Egyptologists have unearthed evidence in which sculptures and wall drawings showed the basic (uncrossed) meditative positions of their ancient peoples. Certainly the ancient Chinese were well aware of and had great respect for this force, this inner strength about which many claims have been made, many true and others perhaps not. Here and now, we shall deal with what we know.

The first attempt at Purposeful Meditation will be referred to as being the First Sitting in order to differentiate from other methods of meditational practice. The First Sitting provides an extremely valuable introduction toward a better and healthier lifestyle. It goes without saying that one should totally refrain from smoking if at all possible. The intake of alcohol prior to the beginning of a sitting would diminish the work and the benefits of it (this of course applies to drugs as well). A very exhausted body should rest and not be engaged in any form of meditation.

**It is also very important to understand that Neo Ch'an Purposeful Meditation bears no similarity to other forms of meditation in that it does not allow the mind to be directed from the outside nor does it permit the mind to wander aimlessly about. This is a crucial and we believe a very important difference especially since we feel you should at all times be in full control of your mind.**

The First Sitting does not concern itself with any other aim than to instill peace and quiet into the mind, to develop good breathing technique while practicing and to gradually spend more time with oneself. During our entire lifetime we might be engaged in many wonderful experiences which seem to aid and benefit the soul; yet, modern recreational practice ensures that man is more active with others than with himself. Our life, which was given free to us, is taken for granted until we learn that it can have limitations. Such limitations present themselves over time in many ways. The ancient masters of the temples knew, by sheer observation and by trial and error, that much of this could be avoided if man could spend time with himself in order to secure a longer and better life. Today, a better life might mean many things to different persons.

Life in its entirety is, however, still connected to a basic quality, meaning: to reach a ripe and old age retaining a clear and workable mind with a well functioning body forfeiting only a certain quickness, the familiar agility one was so accustomed to - a small price to pay for a little time spent with oneself! Of course, meditation alone cannot accomplish all this if the rest of one's activity does not compliment the effort of meditation. In itself, it is quite insignificant. Good eating habits and an all around regimen of exercise are an inseparable part of premeditational practice.

In our modern society, it is conceivable that many individuals never consult their physicians about their activity at all. Your physician has a right to know about your activities or lack of them, whether you meditate. Only he or she is equipped, by the scientific education of a lengthy and serious nature, to know whether the student, having a certain handicap, should in fact train hard and long or practice deep breathing for any length of time. A wide variety of exotic diseases may forbid one or the other method of exercise but usually will never restrict them all. The old masters had an iron rule and they lived by it, telling their students that anything which does not feel good or hurts for any length of time is detrimental to them....and yes, many of these men lived to ages which are not even reached any longer, some Buddhist and Taoist monks are still living today supposedly approaching an estimated two hundred years of age: their lifestyle in all likelihood would be judged to be very boring and uninspiring in comparison to ours. In any event, proof exists that acitvity and rest have a certain common denominator with good food, fresh water and air and that all must be kept in secure balance in order to exact good health.

## A Word about the Fanatic ...

The health fanatic will run many hundreds of miles in a month, pounding the pavement or working to win in a highly paid marathon. He will chase behind the exhaust fumes of the cars on main street in his city because it is there that he will be seen: the side streets are usually never frequented by those persons. He will buy dozens of books and knows more ancient secrets than the ancients themselves: he will consume large quantities of vitamins and meet with "authentic" persons only. Most of these people do not live very long considering their intense efforts and though they appear to look healthy to the rest of us, this is a far cry from the truth. In a free society one can write and publish, speak and teach anything from the most elevating to the most crude and corrupt. At times the books and pamphlets, though they sell by the millions, can be the worst material to rely upon (often stemming from the Orient, the Orient being the source of truth after all!). Salesmanship is not interested in the content but only what the people can be made to think it does for them: this is one reason for the return of medieval practices alike witchcraft and certain branches of medicine which were thought to have disappeared forever, the concept being that all which sells must be good, a process of unlearning or mind-bending:

*so beware and maintain independency of thought.*

# The FIRST SITTING

Before beginning in meditation, Lung One (see Fig. 1-2 at back of this chapter ) and the sitting and standing exercises should be done, neck rotations as well as the known neck turns and lifts (these should be done **very** slowly), resting on one's knees while stretching to the sides forward and backward: the sitting stretches are helpful in order to achieve the necessary physical backing while being in meditation. Do **NOT** do any harsh exercises: all exercises must be kept mild and gentle before a session and only do the exercises which are safe and healthy according to your physical state of health. If you do have any health problems, it is totally your responsibility to govern yourself accordingly.

## The First Practice Session - Indivisual Practice (Fig. 3)

The student assumes the "Ch'i Hu" position in which the right leg crosses in front of the other leg. Observe that the right foot is not placed upon the left thigh.

Since the Neo Ch'an method relies mainly on the lower abdominal region to stimulate the diaphragm, the chest must be well carried in a good sitting posture, allowing for a healthy exchange of the natural fuels. Thus, the posture is of the utmost importance in order to meditate for a certain length of time.

Approaching the ground, the student firstly begins to kneel, then shifting to his left, places his left hand on the ground leaving the left leg bent, crossing the right leg in front of it.

 **NOTE:** You can sit in a chair if you are unable to sit in the above described position.

## Tying the Sash (the Tied Ch'i Hu Position) (Fig. 4)

While stretching forward the sash is being placed high against the lower back above and around the kidney height, well spread and tied far above the right instep running over the thigh of the left resting leg.

> *Observe that the sash is well spread while being looped around the right foot and tied higher up so that the circulation of the blood is not restricted anywhere.* ***THIS IS ABSOLUTELY IMPERATIVE!***

Now, adjust the posture from the bottom up, placing both hands behind you on the ground, lifting the body gently while the buttocks moves not more than two inches backward. The shoulders are kept back and down and the hands placed inward, resting on the far point of the crossed upper portion of your leg, close to the knees. Palms are facing up and the elbows are pointing outward. There may not be any stress exerted by the sash above the kidney zone nor where it crosses the instep of the right leg. Since it does not really hold any part of the body, it appears as if a gentle hand reminds the student to remain at peace while being backed by this invisible hand. This is referred to as the One-sided Position, the Tied Ch'i Hu position.

 **NOTE:** Since people are built differently, it is important to try to come as close to this position as best as your physique and state of health permits and no further.

## The Sitting

The sash being tied as mentioned in the earlier paragraph, it becomes important as to how one begins to assume the correct position for the following practice.

- After sitting down, thrust the buttocks backwards at which time a great deal of comfort should make itself felt. It is much easier now to maintain a position with the **helping hand,** as the sash will appear, pressing mildly into the back area, forcing the buttocks out and away, accenting the normal curvature of the spine. This position of spinal control should also be accepted while walking or sitting in everyday life.

- In performing the first step of the meditative sitting, the hands are now placed on the upper inside of the knee surface, palms upward. The shoulders are kept relaxed and down - but may never curve forward, slouching. Such posture will expose the chest slightly, it will appear well-formed.

- The head is kept straight looking across the room at eye level, concentrating on the center of the Medigraph (Fig. 5 - see back fold out), the smallest but darkest point. The Medigraph has to be at the exact height of the individual's eye level and should be kept approximately five feet away from the person, the only exception being the large version of the Medigraph which is used for an entire class. **Do NOT look down** to the floor or close your eyes, these being other commonly used methods in meditational sittings, but NOT in Neo Ch'an Purposeful Meditation.

- The tongue should rest against the upper palate, head straight and not tilted forward.

Any sitting in the early morning demands a more vigorous form of exercise in order to prepare for meditation since a well rested system will be too sluggish. Morning sittings should never be too lengthy in duration. Your heart rate must not be elevated, however, once you begin the sitting.

With posture correct and feeling at ease, you should now begin the next step.

**BREATHING** The first method of Neo Ch'an breathing is essential in order to train later techniques which assure an overall healthy condition of the lungs, so essential for the exchange of the nourishing gases which the body must take from the air.

In Neo Ch'an Purposeful Meditation one does not breathe from the chest but uses the lower abdomen. Since normal reflexes will partially involve some chest activity while being engaged in inhaling air, one should learn to think downward to where the hands are resting, imagining that one is actually breathing through the exposed palms. The center muscles over the mid-section begin to contract from the top downward forcing air out gently and soundlessly; since the lungs operate in a vacuum-like state the inhaling occurs as an automatic reversal without much effort (Fig. 6).

The inhaling cycle begins by letting the air pass through the nostrils while the mid-section slightly expands: during this period

Fig. 5 - Exhaling

of inhaling one must concentrate not on the chest but very much moreso on the mid-section: on the exhaling cycle it is the muscles of the midsection which should begin to contract from the top downward, thus forcing the air out of the mouth (which should be kept slightly open as soon as the air has passed through the nose downward). At this time, in unison, one should look upon the center of the Medigraph, the dark point and follow the concentric rings to the outside, where the colour gradually begins to become white, blending into nothingness. Do NOT concentrate on the dark center of the Medigraph any longer but leave it, thus advancing to a state where the rings become unimportant, non-existent. Initially this is difficult to do but with practice it will come quite easily.

*Remember: it is easier to concentrate on something than on nothing at all.*

We are now beginning to start concentrating upon something and are trying to enlarge the sphere until the eyes perceive nothing any longer, knowing by mental orientation only that the rings must be still somewhere before us.

### Step One then would be:

Inhale....Focus on the dot.

## Step Two:

The expansion of the focusing, making the eyes follow from the dark to the white, eventually losing the Medigraph from the conscious mind...expansion should be practiced with both eyes wide open (not forcing them extra wide) and relaxing, exhaling as mentioned beforehand.

Since the breathing cycle is connected to the state of mind, one begins to imagine that the breathing originates from the left inside surface of the palm, resting on the left leg. The palms should be turned inward for that purpose. Concentrate on the left palm only while inhaling - not while exhaling.

Remain in that position for a short while, an estimated five minutes or so, not planning to worry about the accuracy of that interval of practice. Do not let the conscious mind be bothered with the keeping of time, since this would definitely distract from the exercise at the outset.

After feeling that a short time has expired, the session should be abandoned in a certain way only. The eyes should begin to catch the Medigraph from the outside first, then proceed to the center, slowly but not in a loitering, time wasting manner.

You have now ended your first session.

Inhale fairly quickly then try to establish a ten second exhaling cycle, five full cycles per minute (leaving about 2 seconds to inhale each time).

*Remember*: all breathing movements must feel good and relaxing and thus if it becomes troublesome to follow a rhythmic cycle in the beginning, it would be wrong to adhere to these five cycles per minute: every human being handles these exercises slightly differently from the next.

 *The aftereffects of a sitting can be:*

*- general soreness in the joints, back; mild discomfort in the mid-section stemming from the contracting and expanding muscles which are normally rarely used as they press against the diaphragm.*

Neo Chan Purposeful Meditation has different stages and levels. Since the Neo Chan breathing method does not work on the chest but rather concentrates on the lower abdomen, the chest still moves noticeably up and down but in time and with practice relinquishes much of its heavy rising and falling motion.

Methods which utilize a staring line, looking upon the ground, have resulted in practitioners experiencing problems concentrating their eyes after meditation. Persons who rely on glasses for better vision should experience on their own whether or not the glasses become a handicap for them. They can be removed if better results are obtained without having them on.

This is the end of the First Sitting of Neo Chan Purposeful Meditation. It must be practiced regularly in order to achieve proficiency. The sitting positions will change as the student begins to advance. The breathing methods will change as the student advances. The general depth of information pertaining to meditation increases while the student practices: advanced methods are introduced only if the student has achieved the previous and essential stages for mind training.

After good skill has been achieved in the practice of the First Sitting, the Second Sitting shall concern itself with the Ch'i breathing while holding a centrally held position differing slightly from the first position.

The Third Sitting shall concern itself with the channelling of the Ch'i energy now developed for the benefit of the practitioner.

The Second Sitting and Third Sitting are not addressed in this book and will be left for a future work. The First Sitting and the process therein is important to develop and thus requires time and effort before the subsequent methods can be practiced with positive results.

◆◆◆ ***The most important point to remember again:*** *in Neo Ch'an Purposeful Meditation you are being trained to control your own mind* **NOT** *to allow it to wander or be controlled by anyone or anything else. This is absolutely crucial in true and healthy meditational practice.*

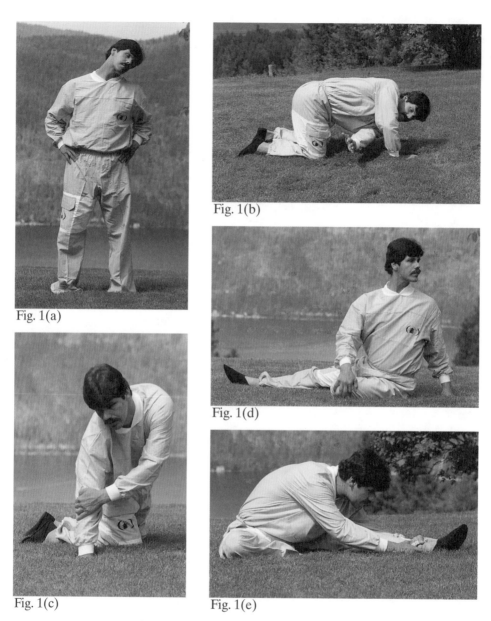

Fig. 1(a)

Fig. 1(b)

Fig. 1(c)

Fig. 1(d)

Fig. 1(e)

## Fig. 1 (a-e) - Pre-stretching exercises

Suggestions only. No stretching should be overdone and all stretches should be done slowly and carefully according to your physical condition and state of health.

# THE TEMPLE SYSTEM

## LUNG 1
### THE DRAGON FORM
Fig. 2

Fig. 2(a)          Fig. 2(b)          Fig. 2(c)

Fig. 2(d)          Fig. 2(e)          Fig. 2(f)

Fig. 2(g)  Fig. 2(h)  Fig. 2(i)

Fig. 2(j)  Fig. 2(k)  Fig. 2(l)

113

Fig. 2(m)  Fig. 2(n)  Fig. 2(o)

Fig. 2(p)  Fig. 2(q)  Fig. 2(r)

114

Fig. 2(s)

Fig. 2(t)

Fig. 2(u)

Fig. 2(v)

Fig. 2(w)

Fig. 2(x)

115

Fig. 3(a)

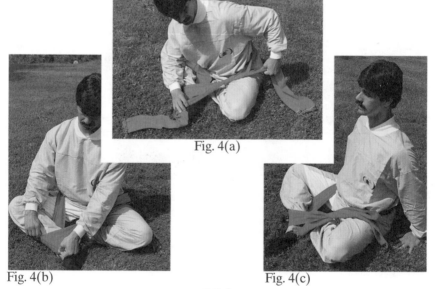

Fig. 4(a)

Fig. 4(b)

Fig. 4(c)

116

# Chapter VIII

♦

# Better Than Motivation, Inspiration

"... It is the power of goodness within us
that makes us succeed lastingly."

Many thinkers throughout the ages had their own distinct outlook on this human capability, that of being able to motivate one's kind for betterment. Schopenhauer arrived at a more plausible explanation as to how he conceived motivation. Motivation incites cause, so he said, sufficient reason toward becoming, knowledge, even being, or action etc. Inspiration, on the other hand, as the Neo Ch'an philosophy sees it, shares the same ground but differs in the spiritual setting of living man. To inspire, the word itself firstly addresses the act of breathing, inhaling, blowing or breathing life into something. Hence, the figurative linguistic derivative to breathe feeling into the soul of a human being, inspiring the soul, an almost supernatural force, **addressing man from within himself through himself**. On the other hand, a motivator might not necessarily inspire while he motivates. Motivation is a rather motive action, at times a repetitive advent used to induce change in human behavior by showing benefit first or gain of some sort, more material in

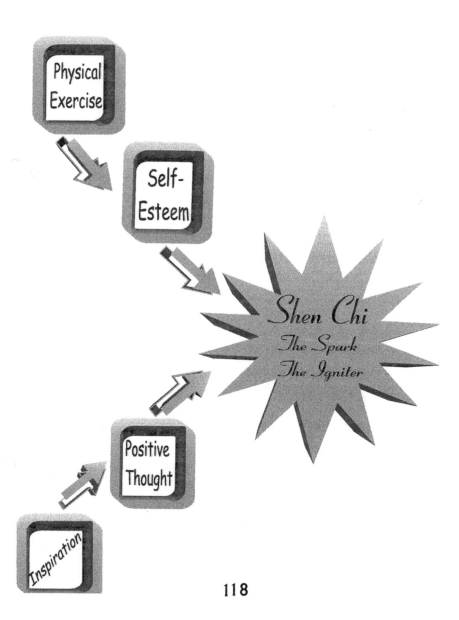

substance than otherwise, in order to get the cooperation of the person to be motivated. Once the motivator leaves, all too often, the motivation expires. **Inspiration, on the other hand, addresses the soul to follow natural laws while elevating human emotion toward reason, thus beginning the path to accept struggle, not luck.** In the Neo Ch'an philosophy reason creates the balancing power for the human mind, inducing emotional intelligence so essential in order to succeed lastingly.

The Neo Ch'an ideal is an attempt to bring about a change within any human being and does, therefore, not anchor itself in the raw concept of motivation but sees its function as offering the natural precepts that allow the human mind and body to induce a change which begins to address mind and body in unison, purifying its powers through P.M., Purposeful Meditation: a concept of mind training which does not please the mind but teaches it to perform, preparing the individual to succeed with awareness. The power of change is not found within the raw onslaught of motivation but rather by concept **through inspiration** which breathes of compassion and understanding for the individual involved in the change toward betterment.

Positive thinking, in itself, does not mean very much unless it can be attached to something which makes such positive thoughts work: alike gasoline, it will become positively active only if it can be ignited. If the spark is missing, the motor will have all the ingredients to run but still cannot begin to turn over. **The positive thought attached to self-esteem begins to cause ignition.**

Something which inspires can ignite the innermost chamber of any human being and overcome almost any handicap or barrier which is made by living man. A false sense of his identity can burden him whereas the right understanding of it will begin to free him from useless and misleading suggestions. Remember: We become what we think about. For this precise reason do we often hear the comment, however, that people are exactly there where they belong which, if well examined, may in fact not be true. Many people accept their position and never bother to move on, to try to get ahead, or better yet, to become independent of unpleasant employment or to learn how to enjoy one's work and succeed in it. This of course depends on the individual and his outlook regarding himself. The most dangerous adventure toward success lies in the attempt to seek out a livelihood to which the person does not bring the essential qualifications. In short: self-honesty will tell whether one should become a mathematician, just because the profession promises a very high salary, when knowingly no such talent exists at all. It can be possible, on the other hand, that someone who in fact hates the subject of physics and mathematics was wrongly introduced to it by a poor teacher and indeed finds out, at a much later time in life, that his true talent had been there all along (Albert Einstein). Many human beings are being misguided by bad experiences and thus are unable to see where the true path toward success really lies. They have no concrete idea of where they are and where they are wishing to go and, if they have an idea, a dream constitutes an idea in itself as well, they have no concept, that is to say no map as to how to arrive there.

Having introduced the philosophy of the Neo Ch'an concept of change, the following outline will summarize the path toward success which I have explained in this book. Each and every human being who ascribes to this path should find a self guarantee toward achievement within it.

Success can mean many things for different persons but inevitably it should relate to a better life, happiness and most of all fulfilment. Here now is the beginning of the path:

## Purposeful Meditation:

*First Mind Training Session*
*- Developing Ch'i energy*

*Second Mind Training Session*
*- Circulating Ch'i energy*

*Third Mind Training Session*
*- To achieve emotional cooperation in order to utilize this new inner strength or Ch'i energy*

## The Path:

- Physical exercise - well balanced, measured, consistent
- Purging of false beliefs, cancelling of failure impulses
- Inspiration leading to positive thinking and enthusiasm, happiness being an internal state of mind as L'Estrange said: *"It is not the place nor the condition but the mind alone that can make anyone either happy or miserable!"*
- Re-affirmation of mind training
- Self-esteem leads to self-confidence through honest and realistic mental picturing
- Insight, self honesty, discipline
- Good planning and timing, reasonable perseverance
- Power of imagination, success being envisioned rationally
- Personality change - feeling and thus emitting positivity to others which eventually results in finding the right assistance, places, financing and/or purpose which then will aid you in fulfilling your goal.

«»«« Swimming Amongst Sharks »»»»

Modern motivation does not concern itself with the individual character of any one human being but sells an idea to all. If we believe that any one human being can be motivated, which is true, it still depends to what degree and how long such motivation, once departed, will last. If you believe that the motivator in question holds the key toward failure and success and he gives this key only to you alone, having knowledge no one else holds, it would be fair to believe that you would have a good chance to succeed over all those who do not have such knowledge. Remember: you will be told again and again that knowledge is power and this alone usually convinces the least educated being that things will begin to change. Be aware, however, that knowledge comes in pairs! There is of course true knowledge, which is truth free of error and there is false knowledge, the lesser type to which one can be easily directed. If now, to make a point, the motivator gives the key to his secrets away to 250 million people, all of them would be as well equipped as you. Since the main motivating force he uses is being based on greed, the path toward success becomes suddenly a very rocky road. It is here where the Neo Ch'an concept begins and some of the modern motivators fail. The final struggle will occur in a pool infested with sharks, each and everyone being highly motivated, ready to outdo, outmanoeuvre and even eliminate any opponent. After all, there is only so much room at the top! Much information is being offered as to how one can succeed matching any and all odds. There are countless works on the market which allude to treachery, telling the reader how one can get what one wants by learning how to intimidate the other human being, simply eliminating him through the right type of maneuver.

We now have arrived on a stage where many of us do not wish to tread; yet, it is not too difficult to **succeed with civility** if one has the right emotional backing and an unbribable character. It is the **power of goodness within us that makes us succeed lastingly** and not the cunning and conniving skills. They lead to rapid success as well as they do invite rapid failure. **It is wise to**

**succeed with people, not over them**! This is our firm belief and it is, therefore, that We have made our concepts public for the very first time: psychological sophrosyne (prudence), proper direction of pursuit, success through the individual by the individual, from the heart and from effort alone, the old-fashioned way, not making money but earning it.

Do not forget this simple truth so readily forfeited and so easily misunderstood as St. Augustus of Hippo said: "**To he who does what in him lies, God will not deny his grace!**"

# Three Tries

Three tries you'll have to make your mark.
Rise with the sun, rest as it goes:
the first attempt to light the dark;
the second stride, amidst all foes

Is perseverance as you struggle on
start over, check your soul and mind.
And least not last if all is gone
do not sell out but seek to find.

Now even if you did all this,
the third most gallant throw
will be a word of love, a kiss
to those who made you go.

Other books by O.E. Simon:

*Adventure Series*:   The White Priest (Vol. I)
                       Takuan the Manchurian (Vol. II)
                       The Tigers of Sinkiang (Vol. III)
                       The Lost Jade (Vol. IV)

*Novels:*              Shalom
                       Curse of the Gods

*Poetry:*              Book of Thought
                       Book of Hope
                       Book of Life
                       Book of Destiny

*Technical Work:*      The Law of the Fist
                       Anti-Rape & Total Self-Defense

Books can be individually ordered from:

> *In Canada*:   Golden Bell Publishing House Inc.
>                P.O. Box 2680
>                Grand Forks, B.C.  V0H 1H0
>
> *In US*:       Golden Bell Publishing House Inc.
>                P.O. Box 181
>                Danville, Washington 99121-0181

or orders may be placed through your local bookstore.

**Note:** *His Holiness does give seminars on Purposeful Meditation and if you wish to attend, you can write to the publisher for his schedule of the city nearest you.*

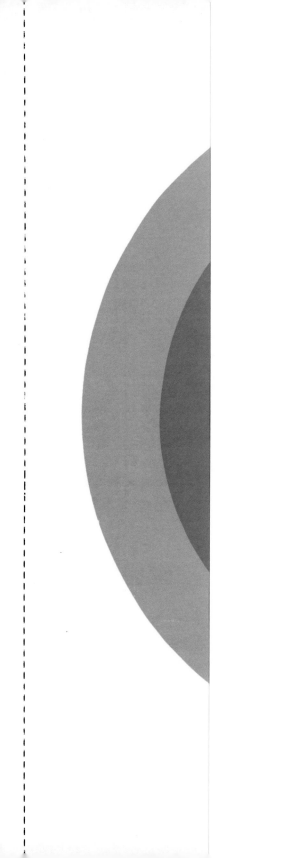